Ballooning

Ballooning

The Complete Guide to Riding the Winds

DICK WIRTH

MAJOR PHOTOGRAPHY BY

JERRY YOUNG

Introduction by Dick Francis

A MARSHALL EDITION FOR

Random House
New York

Edited and designed by
Marshall Editions Ltd,
71 Eccleston Square,
London SW1V 1PJ

Editor: Graeme Ewens
Art Director: Paul Wilkinson
Assistant Editor: John Blackett-Ord

Published in the United States by
Random House Inc., New York and
simultaneously in Canada by Random
House of Canada Ltd, Toronto.

Library of Congress Cataloging in Publication Data
Wirth, Dick.
    Ballooning: The complete guide to riding the wind
    1. Balloon Ascensions—History. I. Young,
Jerry, joint author. II. Title
GV 762.W57   1980   797.5   80–5281
ISBN 0-394-51338-X (hardback)
ISBN 0-394-72796-7 (paperback)

Reproduced by Gilchrist Bros. Ltd, Leeds
Typeset by Vantage, Southampton
Printed and bound in Spain by
Printer industria gráfica sa
Sant Vicenç dels Horts,
Barcelona
D.L.B. 11543-1980

Massed ascension at Albuquerque, New Mexico

BALLOONIST'S MAKE BETTER LOVERS

Contents

Introduction

I first fell in love with hot-air balloons when I was invited to see the beginning of a balloon race at Longleat, in Wiltshire. Those gorgeous, brilliant, floating fantasies—I would have sailed off with them straight away if anyone had offered.

On the next evening I went to the balloonists' gala dinner and watched the trophies being presented to the winners, and what struck me most was the intensity of the joy which this sport spread in its competitors.

Since then I've been up there, travelling on the wind with my wife and a professional balloon pilot. In 1978 when I was writing *Whip Hand*, which features a balloon race, Julian Nott generously brought a balloon to our house and lifted us out of our fields.

As an ex-fighter and bomber pilot myself I feel (not surprisingly) at home in the air, but what ballooning especially does is to stretch time out and let one see new slants on old things. The earth itself looks different, the shape of the past showing markedly under the fields of the present; and one's view of the world mellows and slows. Ballooning brings tranquillity to the soul—with minor exceptions like when the fuel is running out, there's a gale blowing up or a tree tears the fabric.

The yearning to lift off to the high blue yonder must be basic in human nature because the search for means of flight has been so universal, so ingenious, and so stubbornly persistent. This book is fascinating about history, technically informative and beautiful to look at. But for the deepest insight of all into the subject—go for a ride!

Dick Francis

The magic of flying

> '...a calm delight which is inexpressible and which no situation on earth could give.'
>
> *Lunardi's Account.*

Hot air is my way of life. I float in the clouds and ride with the wind. I have access to a God-given tranquillity and to an adventure that can be chillingly frightening.

I have been totally committed since my first flight in 1971. To be consumed by a passion for lighter-than-air travel places one apart from the majority of earthbound 'pedestrian' mortals, with their different values. While driving through the countryside, others might notice quaint villages and expansive vistas but, as a balloonist, I see the landscape as a series of good or bad launch and landing sites. The countryside is a rich source of airfields for 'balloonatics'—any uninhabited field, screened from the wind by trees, provides us with easy access to the sky.

Balloons take you out of this world in the most graceful style. To float away in one is to realize the common fantasy of living in the clouds. Just a few feet off the Earth's surface the restraints of daily life are already left behind. The gentle lifting motion is accompanied by a rapid change of perspective as trees drop away and waving figures diminish. The sound of the burner heating the air in the envelope is an intrusion, but it is in direct response to the pilot's control and for the serenity it provides the blast is a minor inconvenience; in fact, the noise is a vital accompaniment because, as all hot-air balloonists are aware, the time to worry is when the noise stops.

Direction depends on the wind, but the powerful gas burners of modern balloons allow the pilot complete control of his vertical movement.

Hot-air ballooning is the answer to a primal fantasy made possible by high technology. Gas ballooning is, by comparison, something of an anachronism. Bags of ballast and trailing drag ropes have no place in a manoeuvrable, hot-air balloon. Hot air is, of course, gas but, unlike hydrogen, it is inert and cheap. The two aspects of 'aerostation' (the science and art of lighter-than-air flight) do have many similarities but hot-air balloons are more easily available and more responsive than gas balloons and they do not need complex refuelling facilities.

By applying the principle that hot air rises, the modern-day balloonist ascends rapidly into the blue yonder with many millions of BTUs (units of thermal energy) at his disposal. To moderate the rate of climb, which can be up to 2,000 feet per minute (25 mph) or to descend, a vent in the balloon envelope can be opened. Once the hot, thin air escapes, the craft begins to drop. A further blast on the heater will stabilize the balloon. Experienced balloonists can fly to within inches of a desired height, balancing a craft with a mass of four tons or more by delicate fingertip control. Through subtle changes in altitude pilots can 'steer' their craft to a limited degree and flights can be planned to use the predictable changes of wind direction at various heights.

There are general principles which cover the global wind patterns but it is by using the effects of macro- and micro-climate that controlled navigation is possible. The wind direction above a pilot's flight level is often difficult to predict. In the northern hemisphere it should swing a balloon to the right as height is gained but this is by no means consistent, and weather forecasts are of little use in micro-climate conditions. It is possible to see the movement of clouds above and often this is the only guide to conditions at greater altitude.

The wind direction below is easier to deduce. There may be clouds beneath but if not there are wind direction sensors to be found in most landscapes: in winter the smoke from domestic fires; in summer wind-rippled crops, the waves on lakes and laundry hanging in gardens.

The ability to read these signs and ride the winds is a skill required of competitive balloonists, but when man is out of his own element there is only a limited contribution he can make. The random nature of the destination is one of the major attractions to the average aeronaut. His destiny is written in the wind.

Once airborne, the balloon basket becomes an unearthly lookout post. As its distorted shadow floats at a leisured pace across the meadows below, a balloon is in harmony with the flow of natural forces. From this perspective balloonists begin to view the landscape for its beauty rather than for its suitability for take-off or landing.

Clear sky and clear heads: conditions for ballooning are usually best in the early morning. The New Mexico sun has been up for five minutes, the pilots for an hour.

From their privileged position balloonists can study earth-bound sportsmen, like the English bowls players (bottom right), most of whom are unaware of the high fliers overhead.

Balloon designs range from the spectacularly individual to the proudly patriotic. The striped balloon has been set rocking by a mid-air collision with one in Australian colours.

Balloon flight controls are so simple to operate that one quickly feels relaxed in the air. Exhilaration comes from the feeling that control is a simple matter of will-power and most of the time is spent quietly observing the tableau beneath. Any landscape, however familiar, can take the breath away when viewed from this angle. The bird's-eye view is a flattering one. Seen in the context of a vast panorama, country towns lose their self-importance, main streets are seen as through-routes calmly linking horizons. Natural topography provides shelter for small, cosy villages, farms nestle in the valleys and grand houses stand proud on prominent hill tops.

Lakes, things of beauty from any angle, take on new dimensions as a balloon slowly floats across. Sky merges with water, reflection with reality, and the coloured globe hangs quietly over the water until a gust of wind ripples the surface and wafts the balloon away.

The patterns of nature, the dependence on the seasons and the relationships between neighbouring communities can be seen so clearly as to suggest that the whole grand design could only have been laid out from above. The salutary effect of this experience on a basket-borne observer is to make the troubles of the world invisible. Things look right. There is a sense of proportion and man, far from feeling superior and above it all, can only be made to feel rightfully small—not insignificant, but in proportion to the whole Earth curving away beneath him.

Like the underwater environment, the lower atmosphere can hypnotize its occupants with its calm. Floating on the breeze gives little sensation of gaining ground. Speed is relative to the passage of landmarks beneath and, unless the wind is fresh, progress is gentle. There is no friction and no resistance to the currents of the wind. Everything which floats in the breeze does so at the same speed: balloons keep pace with windborne seeds of dandelions and smoke from chimneys. Up here direction, distance and other terrestrial considerations have no meaning. The tracking is left to the retrieve crew who, every pilot hopes, will be following directly beneath.

As they gain altitude, aeronauts become progressively disengaged from the influences of the earth below. The air becomes colder, cleaner and thinner. The shadows on the landscape

Inflated balloons provide a canopy of shade. Smoke flares may be used as wind indicators, or just to add atmosphere. The 'pompier', with aerostat reflected in his helmet, stands by in case of danger. In some places, the law decrees that firemen must be present at hot inflations.

gradually lose contrast until, eventually, the whole takes on a misty, shrouded appearance, details becoming indistinguishable. Attention is now directed upwards, until the mists of the cloud layer fold around the basket.

When the cloud layer is penetrated, the undiffused light of the sun dazzles unprotected eyes and the crazy-foam piles of clouds reflect the sun's brilliance back into the deep blue. Balloonists don't live with their heads in the clouds; they prefer to stand in them.

As it plunges downwards through the clouds, the balloon is enveloped in a haze of crystals which shimmer and sparkle before they fuse into the damp, cold mist. Within this clammy embrace all sounds are magnified. The constant hiss of the pilot flame, uninterrupted by the roar of the burner, reminds the aeronauts that they are descending at the speed of an elevator. When it matters, a balloon can be induced to drop at 2,000 fpm, shaking and turning as it gathers speed.

And then, suddenly, the first smudgy colours of the countryside become visible. Shooting out through the ceiling, the balloon returns to the comparatively featureless light of the mundane, real world.

The most testing part of any flight, whether by glider, Concorde or balloon, is the landing. Only balloonists suffer the ignominy of being dragged across the ground in what is virtually a laundry basket—but even rough landings rarely deter people from wanting to fly again.

As soon as the wickerwork touches dirt, the pilot pulls his rip line. The envelope, which moments previously was holding the occupants in delicate suspension, is now distorted, its form torn open by the rip line, the perfect symmetry destroyed. As the warm, propane-smelling air spills back into the sky, the balloon's identity fades. Its coloured segments, stripes and sponsor's message collapse and the basket which has been dragged behind slows to a halt. The occupants slide, fall or roll out, like rag dolls from a toy box, moving disjointedly, speaking in grunts, not yet re-adjusted to the real world.

Under ideal conditions, a balloon will be lowered gracefully into a dry, unoccupied field, coming to a gradual halt close to a road. But I have landed in barbed wire at 50 mph and in a zone filled with flying lead from the guns of enthusiastic hunters. My balloon has been

Photographer Jerry Young utilizes ultra-wide angle and fisheye lenses for all-embracing views of the sky—from ground level and at 10,000 ft.

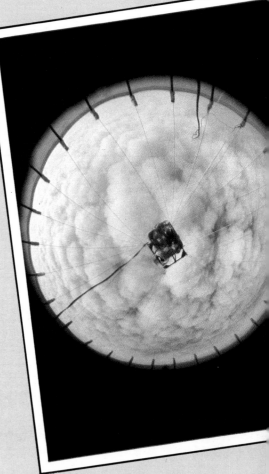

followed by inquisitive motorists across fields of precious crops, and I have been accused of frightening a pig to death (although the pig stopped playing dead before charges were pressed).

While ballooning is a tranquil pursuit there is always an element of danger giving an edge to the pleasure. Ballooning is not blood and guts but it is demanding in a way which stimulates every sense, providing a satisfaction such as no other I have experienced.

I have known real fear in the air, for a balloon responds to the atmosphere, not always to the pilot. High winds make for exciting flights and bone-rattling landings, and at times I have wondered whether I would set unbroken foot back on the earth. Out of sight of land, hidden by mist, there are powerful forces that can send a balloon gyrating helplessly in crazy switch-back spasms. At such times my decisions are critical. Then I come to know myself a little better. Ballooning is frequently a real test of that indefinable inner self.

There is no real *reason* to be up there, caught in an updraught, driven higher and higher over the formidable Alps, or blown towards a coastline and the last chance of a dry landing, or becalmed over a lake, running out of fuel. Only a balloon, a machine which goes readily up and down but only grudgingly left and right, could get you into situations like that. Only the reactions of an aeronaut and the compliance of fate can get you out.

I do not have to fly at great altitude to enjoy my ballooning. There is satisfaction in flying low, cruising over a wheatfield, perhaps only inches above the rippling crop, floating smoothly and controlling the balloon, with bursts of flame, to follow the contours of the land. I delight in the power which this monstrous piece of equipment affords me.

Faced with a difficult choice to make during a competition, such as having to decide at what point to descend from several thousand feet, my mind can become crystal clear in a way that it never is on the ground. My body can feel the finest vibrations, the subtlest movement of the balloon, while I concentrate on the invisible pathway down, through emptiness, to a point on the ground.

Balloonists are a privileged group who hold the franchise on low cost, three-dimensional

A balloonist's view of the desert is not obscured by the dust which bedevils land based expeditions. The exaggerated camel shapes are actually long shadows thrown by the afternoon sun.

recreation, but I am especially fortunate in being a professional aeronaut. With my partners at Thunder Balloons, I am able to conceive, design and construct my own machines. One of the most satisfying of our recent projects was the development of a one-man balloon, now known as the Sky Chariot. There have previously been several 'solo' balloons made in America and Britain, but there were no production types generally available.

The Chariot pilot sits across, not astride, the fuel tank, strapped to a back rest. As his legs are dangling in front, the only safe way to land is backwards—so the envelope is fitted with vents which allow the balloon to be rotated.

As designer and, therefore, test pilot, I was the first to be strapped into the Chariot, on New Year's Day 1980. Charged with the expectancy which must fill all aircraft builders, I lifted off in a keen wind to put my new toy to the test. To an experienced balloonist, whose second home is a wicker basket, the feeling of hanging, dangling the feet, spinning slowly, was a new liberation. After a $12\frac{1}{2}$-minute flight I was delighted at the potential of the balloon as a means of even easier access to the sky.

The Chariot is like an aerial motorcycle; it is manoeuvrable, responsive and as presumptuous as a motorized trapeze. It is an air toy with the altitude and endurance capabilities of a conventional balloon. Personal ballooning is here to stay.

The freedom of the air, the excitement of facing danger and the joy which comes from a new viewpoint on beauty are some of the attractions of ballooning. Yet it would be wrong to suggest that the appreciation of natural beauty and the knowledge of oneself, gained through extremes of fear and happiness, are more than elements in the total delight of flying a balloon. Ballooning is addictive. But it is not just an activity for loners. Ballooning is a sport and contact with other balloonists, especially friendly competition, is an important aspect. In what other sport could groups of 50 or more people be found in a grassy field, before the sun has risen, looking towards the sky and preparing to grab at it? The bond of ballooning is strong.

The sport takes place in some beautiful locations, which provide a background to the social activities. I have flown over the Kenyan bush, the Swiss Alps, the deserts of Morocco and Egypt, the valleys of the Loire, the orange groves of California and the frozen wastes of northern Sweden. I relish the friendships I have made in Athens and Paris and Albuquerque and Vienna, consolidated in those hours of balloon talk when the weather was not 'flyable'.

Among earth-bound people, balloonists are welcome enough. Their eye-catching craft are enthralling to watch and the landings bring touches of excitement to tranquil settings. The image lingers in the mind longer than the balloon hangs in the air. The image is a seductive one: it *is* possible to float in the clouds.

The dreams of flight can be realized and a person who has experienced the magic of floating on the breeze will be enchanted. There are very few ex-balloonists.

Balloonists who express their personalities with flamboyant envelope designs can often be recognized on the ground by an obvious passion for badges. The man with 'balloon' tyres on his motorcycle is a security guard at the Albuquerque launch site.

Contrasting aspects of aerostation; balloon and sun rise together through the dust of Kenya's Masai Mara; the hectic scene from a British competition meet hints at the drama to be found during inflation and take-off—metamorphic moments when plastic bags become graceful cloud cruisers.

Aiming for the heavens

'When the mortals go cloud soaring . . . they sit cross-legged and rise straight from that position.'

Monkey.

In ancient times the search for the secret of flight absorbed the most intelligent and inventive minds. Artefacts of long-dead cultures, fragments of clay, wood and metal, show the machines that were the space fiction of their age.

Myth and reality are often confusedly jumbled in accounts from pre-Christian societies but, if certain legends are to be trusted, the principles of flight were understood and perhaps put into practice early in history. The precious knowledge was lost and it took thousands of years to rediscover it. Documentary evidence supports many theories but the proof of man's ability to defy gravity is only 200 years old.

The early attempts at flight were often motivated more by a desire to reach the gods, and even to absorb their power, than to use their backyard as a playground. In Greek, Roman, Norse, Indian, American-Indian, Chinese and other legends, man tries every imaginable means of flying.

Most of the accounts of ancient attempts to fly document a fascination with ornithomorphic or birdlike principles. Thanks to their muscle deployment birds are able to use the aerodynamic properties of their wings to gain lift. Man has yet to imitate their action successfully, but several fanciful designs survive which show birds harnessed to aerial carriages.

The legend of Daedalus and Icarus, who fabricated birdlike wings and flew over the Aegean Sea, provides a perfect realization of the fantasy of personal flight, but we know that in reality they could not have succeeded. Rather than trying to imitate the flight of birds it was to those other occupants of the sky, the floating clouds, that man should have looked for inspiration.

It now seems, however, that some ancient civilizations did realize that harnessing smoke, which can be seen to rise, was a more plausible way of taking to the air than trying to imitate the complex muscular mechanism that enables birds to fly.

Certainly in the Chinese legend *Monkey* (a version of which, based on an earlier source, was published in the fourteenth century), the eponymous hero flies on a cloud—a variation on the magic carpet that suggests an awareness of the lighter-than-air theory of flight. Apparently the ancient Chinese were not as disapproving of attempts to travel with the gods as Europeans often were, but there were reasons to take to the air other trying to reach heaven. There are accounts from the Yin dynasty (twelfth century BC) of man-carrying balloons (possibly smoke-

（氣球證天）

氣的用項最大　譬如一氣球
那球中也純是氣做成的
若球一破　那氣便散開
不能上升了　西人每以氣球
比天　天體渾圓　大氣包旋
日月五星　地球萬物　都被
這大氣吸住　所以各行各的
軌道　一穿　地球吸往
球一穿　大氣漏洩　那地球
日球　月球　都落在一處
不能行動了　有氣　然後
能生力　氣學員真是要緊的

This page from a Chinese book refers to an early 'western' theory that the universe is like a balloon. If it is pierced the gas will escape and sun, moon, earth and stars will cease to move.
The Chinese themselves have been flying paper lanterns for several hundred years—a custom which continues at 'Kung Min' festivals to this day. The traditional Chinese lantern is almost identical in construction to the device we recognize as the first to lift a person off the ground.

Cyrano de Bergerac's hero was carried aloft by flasks of dew worn on his belt. Lana-Terzi's design (left) was theoretically sound but lack of suitable materials kept it on the ground.

powered) and it has been suggested that these might have been used for observation in warfare.

Useful scientific principles survived from several civilizations to inspire future experimenters. Archimedes stated before 200 BC that when a body is immersed in a fluid its loss of weight is equal to the weight of the fluid it displaces. Some 1800 years later Galileo showed that air is a fluid with a calculable weight. In the meantime a thirteenth-century Franciscan monk, Roger Bacon, had constructed hollow globes which he filled with 'aetherial air'. The contained cloud was coming closer.

The French writer Cyrano de Bergerac, active at the time Galileo was developing his theories, wrote a fantasy about travels to the moon and sun in which he proposed that his hero should fly through space 'held aloft by flasks of vaporous dew' which would become lighter in the heat of the sun—a theory which might eventually have led him to invent a solar-powered hot-air balloon.

Scientific progress continued on several fronts. The German Guernicke, whose 'Magdeburg semi-spheres', enclosing a vacuum, constituted the first air-pump, inspired a Jesuit priest, Francesco de Lana-Terzi, to propose a feasible balloon theory.

Lana-Terzi's design, published in 1670, was for a wooden ship lifted by four spheres of thin copper sheet. The spheres, which were to have been evacuated of air, would have weighed less than the air they displaced. In fact, the spheres could not have been built strongly enough to resist the forces of the vacuum but the thesis titillated the scientific world. The idea of floating rather than flapping at last gained general currency but, in the context of Renaissance technology, flying of any kind remained scientific fiction.

In 1709 Bartolemeu de Gusmao, a Brazilian priest, demonstrated a model hot-air balloon to Johan V of Portugal, who was inspired to finance the *Passarola* (*Great Bird*). This was to have been a passenger-carrying version of the model, but there is no record of a successful flight.

By the mid-eighteenth century, the search was on for the basic atomic structure of the universe and in 1776, while experimenting with various gases, Henry Cavendish discovered 'inflammable air', now known as hydrogen, which weighed less than air.

Cavendish's achievement undoubtedly stimulated the minds of frustrated aeronauts everywhere. Hot air was a possible medium, but this new gas, seven times lighter than air, was a scientific certainty.

Aerostation was to soon become a reality, but for the next seven years a technological problem persisted—how to make a fabric to contain the gas. Once this had been solved there were some second thoughts about fulfilling the dream. Might there be some awful fate awaiting humans above the clouds? The makers of the first aerostats sent up animals, most of which seem to have survived their landings to run away.

EXPRIENCE AROSTATIQUE FAITE VERSAILLES LE 19 SEPT. 1783

Once he had the means to fly man had second thoughts about his safety. Although the Montgolfiers had intended a man to make the first flight, Louis XVI decreed that animals should take the risk. A sheep, a duck and a rooster became the first European air travellers in 1783.

Even after manned ascents had been made, de Bergerac's influence persisted. This engraving from 1784 shows the use of hydrogen floats attached to clothing like life-preservers.

Two hundred years of flight

The Montgolfier brothers were paper makers who discovered balloons while looking for applications for their product. Their first balloon, made of paper and light fabric, had been seen to rise when held over an open fire in June 1783. Following uncrewed test flights, animals were sent up on tethered ascensions, and finally human beings. These first balloon flights engendered great excitement. It is reported that a crowd of 400,000 attended the first launch in the Bois de Boulogne—virtually the entire population of Paris at that time. The two men had to constantly feed their greedy fire with straw and sheep's wool while dousing the fires started by sparks in the papers and silks of their frail craft. They narrowly avoided an unplanned landing in the Rue de Sèvres by forcing their primitive fire.

Twenty-five minutes after take-off the two aeronauts came softly to earth. The timelessness of ballooning is reflected in d'Arlandes' comment that 'the silence surrounding us surprised me'. He had discovered the addiction which still consumes all balloonists.

The second manned flight, by J.A.C. Charles on December 1, exhibited more technical competence and design knowledge than that of his rivals. The Charlière was a gas (hydrogen) type and in its first flight from the Tuileries gardens in Paris it covered 27 miles, climbed to an altitude of 820 ft and stayed in the air for more than $2\frac{1}{2}$ hours. Charles made his first landing, dropped his passenger, Professor Robert, and took off again.

Flying solo in the gathering dusk, he rose to some 9,000 ft to sight his second sunset of the day.

First manned Montgolfière 1783

Unmanned Montgolfière 1783

Charlière 1783

1783

The race to be the first to fly was a close-run thing. After centuries of imaginative effort had been expended in the search for the secret of flight, the first two manned flying machines lifted off within days of each other, both from French soil.

On November 21, 1783, a young physicist, Jean-François Pilâtre de Rozier, and an army major, the

Marquis François d'Arlandes, rose into the sky before Louis XVI and Marie Antoinette. Their flight in the Montgolfier brothers' balloon was short (25 minutes) and at little more than walking speed, but it was the first free flight. The Montgolfier

brothers of Annonay had beaten Professor J.A.C. Charles of the Académie Française in the race to put men into the sky.

Lunardi's first flight in Britain 1784

Lunardi's second flight 1785

1784

Joseph Montgolfier's only flight was in *Le Fleusselles*, an enormous balloon with a passenger capacity in excess of 30. If the accounts of the time are correct, it was the largest man-carrying hot-air balloon ever built. And it will probably remain so. With a volume of 20,000m³, or 700,000 cu ft, it must have dwarfed every building in Lyon, from where the ascent was made on January 19, 1784.

The first balloon ascent outside France took place in London on September 15, 1784, 10 months after the initial success in Paris. A minor Italian diplomat, Vincent Lunardi, took off from the grounds of the Honourable Artillery Company near Moorfields. (By chance this site is little more than 200 yards from Thunder Balloons' workshop.) His balloon contained 18,200 cu ft of hydrogen. A crowd of 100,000 people, including the Prince of Wales, watched the launch. In 1 hour 40 minutes Lunardi flew to North Mimms—a distance of approximately 13 miles—where he landed, rose again and finally touched down at Long Mead, near Ware in Hertfordshire. Londoners greeted him as a hero, and he was presented to George III. Lunardi continued his ballooning career in England until the death of one of his crew in 1786 made him unpopular. He fled the country and returned to Europe where he continued flying until his death in 1806.

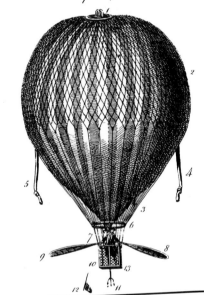

The ENGLISH BALLOON and Appendages in which *Mr* LUNARDI *ascended into the Atmosphere from the Artillery Ground, Sepr 15 1784.*

AN

ACCOUNT

OF THE

First Aërial Voyage in *England.*

AN ACCOUNT

OF THE

FIRST AËRIAL VOYAGE

in *ENGLAND.*

LETTER I.

My Honoured Friend,   *London, July 15, 1784.*

THE innumerable inſtances of kindneſs I have received from you, and the reſpectful affection impreſſed on my mind, have inſenſibly led me into the habit of giving all my intereſting thoughts and actions, ſome reference to you; and making your opinion and ſatisfaction neceſſary to my happineſs.

You are well apprized of the general effect which the attempts to perform Aërial Voyages in France, have had in Europe; but you may not know, that the Philoſophers in England have attended to them with a ſilence, and apparent indifference, not eaſily to be accounted for.

B   Theſe

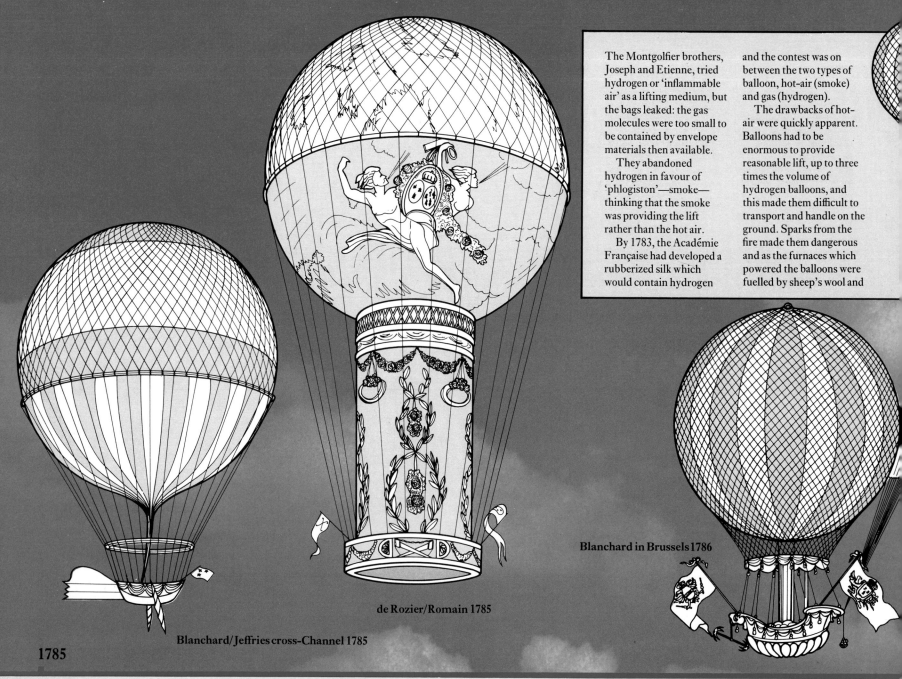

The Montgolfier brothers, Joseph and Etienne, tried hydrogen or 'inflammable air' as a lifting medium, but the bags leaked: the gas molecules were too small to be contained by envelope materials then available.

They abandoned hydrogen in favour of 'phlogiston'—smoke— thinking that the smoke was providing the lift rather than the hot air.

By 1783, the Académie Française had developed a rubberized silk which would contain hydrogen and the contest was on between the two types of balloon, hot-air (smoke) and gas (hydrogen).

The drawbacks of hot-air were quickly apparent. Balloons had to be enormous to provide reasonable lift, up to three times the volume of hydrogen balloons, and this made them difficult to transport and handle on the ground. Sparks from the fire made them dangerous and as the furnaces which powered the balloons were fuelled by sheep's wool and

Blanchard in Brussels 1786

de Rozier/Romain 1785

Blanchard/Jeffries cross-Channel 1785

1785

The next great adventure after that of flying itself was to cross the English Channel. In 1785 the Frenchman Jean-Pierre Blanchard attempted the crossing with Dr. John Jeffries, the first American to fly.

It is reported that Blanchard tried to convince Jeffries (who had paid more than £700 for the preparations) that the balloon had insufficient lift to carry both of them. Jeffries, however, was not deceived and persuaded the Frenchman to remove his lead-weighted belt. The pair took off in a light north-westerly wind and reached France some 2½ hours later, having thrown overboard all their ballast, most of their clothes and every loose item in the basket other than the first airmail letter.

Six months after Blanchard's crossing, the world's first airman, de Rozier, attempted a channel crossing from Boulogne to England in an aerostat which combined hot air and hydrogen. A gas-filled sphere, 30 ft in diameter, sat atop a hot air-filled cylinder some 12 ft in diameter and 21 ft high. The craft was a forerunner of machines which have recently attempted the Atlantic crossing—but it contained inflammable gas and not the inert helium currently in use. The launch went well, but the wind reversed at altitude and turned the balloon back towards France. Disaster struck as either an electrical discharge or a simple spark from the craft's fire ignited the envelope. Within seconds the balloon was shrouded in smoke and, as the flames reached the hydrogen, the two aeronauts plummeted to the ground. Both de Rozier and his employee-passenger, Romain, were killed. Thus the first man to fly was the first to die in an air crash.

Jean-Pierre Blanchard was the first professional aeronaut. He filled the years from 1785 until the French Revolution in 1789 with tireless balloon promotion, introducing aerostats into Holland, Belgium, Germany, Poland, Czechoslovakia, Switzerland and finally the USA.

The revolution and the uncertainties in Europe

damp straw, a foul-smelling, acrid smoke choked the crew. Finally, the flight duration of hot-air balloons was limited by fuel supplies. The hot-air balloon was an anachronism at birth and it soon went out of favour, a process hastened by the disaster in which Pilâtre de Rozier lost his life.

From the beginning the military potential of balloons as espionage platforms was understood in France, whose armed adventures were a large part of national life at the time. The gas balloon was well suited for this purpose: it could stay aloft and still for long periods while the aeronaut devoted himself to observation; and its smallness made it less susceptible to buffeting in high winds. Scientists, too, could use these capabilities for observations at altitude.

So the hot-air balloon, centre of the 1960s renaissance, was only rarely found between 1800 and 1960. For 160 years gas balloons reigned supreme.

Madame Blanchard celebrates Napoleon's marriage 1810

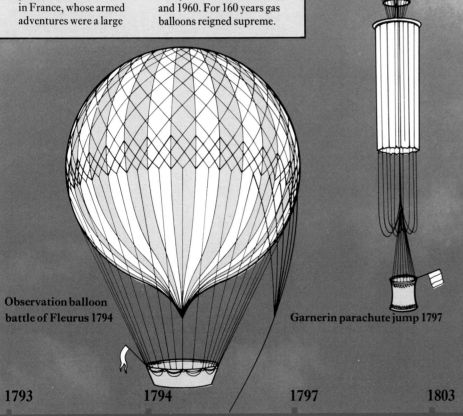

Observation balloon battle of Fleurus 1794

Garnerin parachute jump 1797

1793	1794	1797	1803	1804	1810

drove Blanchard and his aeronaut wife to America where he made the first balloon ascent on the continent on January 9, 1793, at Philadelphia in the presence of George Washington himself. In 1808 he made his last balloon flight, hot-air this time, during which he suffered a fatal heart attack. It was his sixtieth voyage.

Although Blanchard had descended from his balloon by parachute as early as 1785 it was another Frenchman, A. J. Garnerin, master showman, balloonist and adventurer, who perfected the parachute. On October 22, 1797, he made his first fall, from an altitude of less than 3,000 ft in a small basket under a 36 ft-diameter parachute.

Etienne Robertson is reported to have reached an altitude in excess of 23,000 ft on an ascent from Hamburg. Robertson, a Belgian professor, was also to make Copenhagen's first manned flight, in 1806. His son Eugene later made ascents in the USA.

Jacques Garnerin, ever the showman, suggested that Napoleon's coronation be celebrated by a balloon ascent. To the delight of the Parisian crowd the unmanned balloon, ablaze with coloured lights, rose from the city. But Garnerin lost his job as leader of the flying corps when news that the balloon had crashed into a statue of Nero outside Rome was interpreted by Napoleon as a personal insult and a bad omen.

Joseph Gay-Lussac claimed to have reached an altitude of about 21,000 ft and recorded scientific observations on the reactions of birds and animals to the thin atmosphere. He also studied the nature of the Earth's magnetic field at altitude.

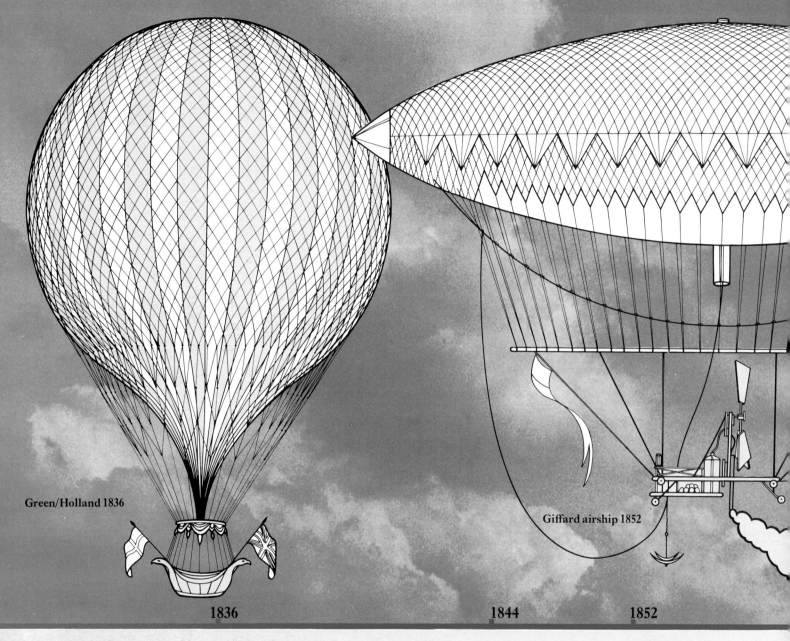

Green/Holland 1836

Giffard airship 1852

1825   **1836**   **1844**   **1852**

The Robertsons were a family of balloon pioneers. The father, Etienne, held altitude records in Europe and one son, Dimitri, launched the first balloon in India. In 1825 another son, Eugène Robertson, made the first ascent from New York, at a celebration for the Marquis de Lafayette, the Frenchman who had endeared himself to Americans as a champion of their Revolution. A year later Eugène reached 21,000 ft, an American altitude record.

The place to be seen in London on a summer evening 150 years ago was Vauxhall Gardens. In September 1836 the pleasure park's spectacular entertainments reached a new height: 13,000 ft. An aeronaut named Charles Green ascended in the 70,000 cu ft *Royal Vauxhall*. Two months later Green, with two companions, travelled farther by air than anyone before him. *Royal Vauxhall* was renamed *Nassau*, in honour of the German duchy in which it landed, 480 miles from home.

'Astounding news! By express via Norfolk: The Atlantic crossed in three days! Signal triumph of Mr. Monck Mason's flying machine'. Thus read headlines in the *New York Sun*, April 13. Edgar Allen Poe, then a struggling reporter, was exercising his talent for fiction. The story was a hoax.

The French engineer Henri Giffard is usually credited with building the first dirigible, an elegantly shaped ovoid 144 ft long and 40 ft in diameter. It had a volume of 88,287 cu ft, providing enough lift to carry a gondola and engine suspended on a pole beneath.

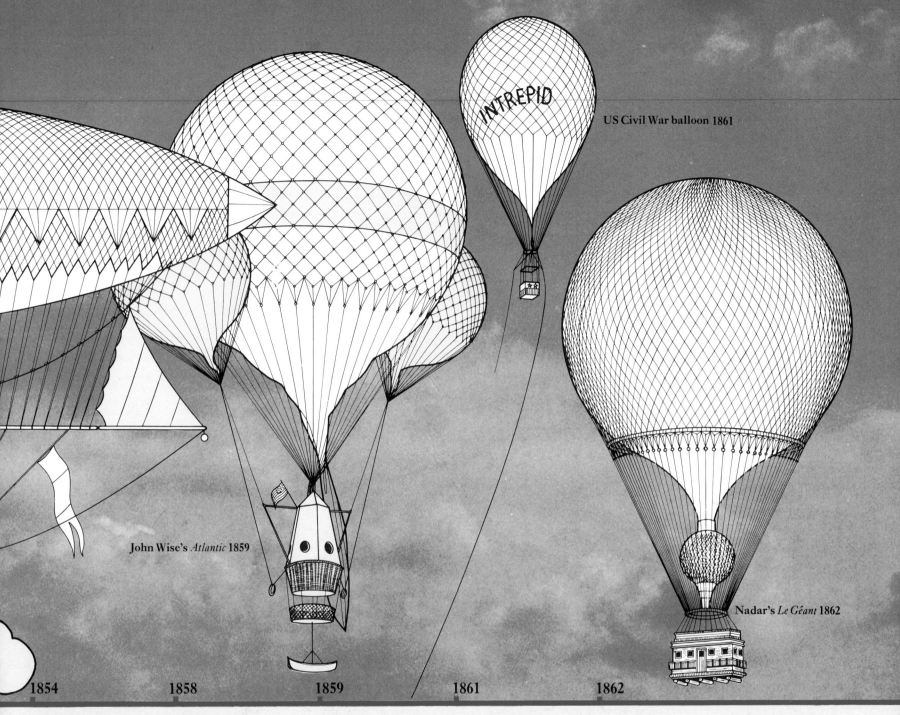

INTREPID

US Civil War balloon 1861

John Wise's *Atlantic* 1859

Nadar's *Le Géant* 1862

1854	1858	1859	1861	1862

Francois Letour was killed when experimenting with a glider take-off from a balloon, at the Cremorne Gardens in London.

1857

Félix du Temple, a French naval officer, built a steam-driven model aircraft which took off and landed under its own power.

Félix Nadar took the world's first aerial photograph from a balloon over Paris.

Probably the greatest aeronaut of all time was John Wise. Only three months after his first flight he invented the rip panel. He developed a theory that winds at altitude are constant and predictable. His balloon *Atlantic* was built to use these 'jet streams' on transoceanic journeys. On a test run he travelled 1,200 miles, from St Louis to Lake Ontario.

Tethered balloons were used by both sides during the American Civil War. In 1861 Thaddeus Lowe, on observation duties, dispatched the first aerial telegram. By December of that year the Union balloon corps had seven balloons in commission.

British meteorologist James Glaisher and his co-pilot, Henry Coxwell, soared to over 29,000 ft above Wolverhampton. During an epic flight they suffered hypoxia, the effects on the body and mind of oxygen starvation.

Nadar's balloon *Le Géant* flew for the first time. It had a volume of 212,000 cu ft and a capacity to lift over 4 tons. On its second flight the balloon was blown out of control but the occupants escaped injury and the envelope was repaired to be used again.

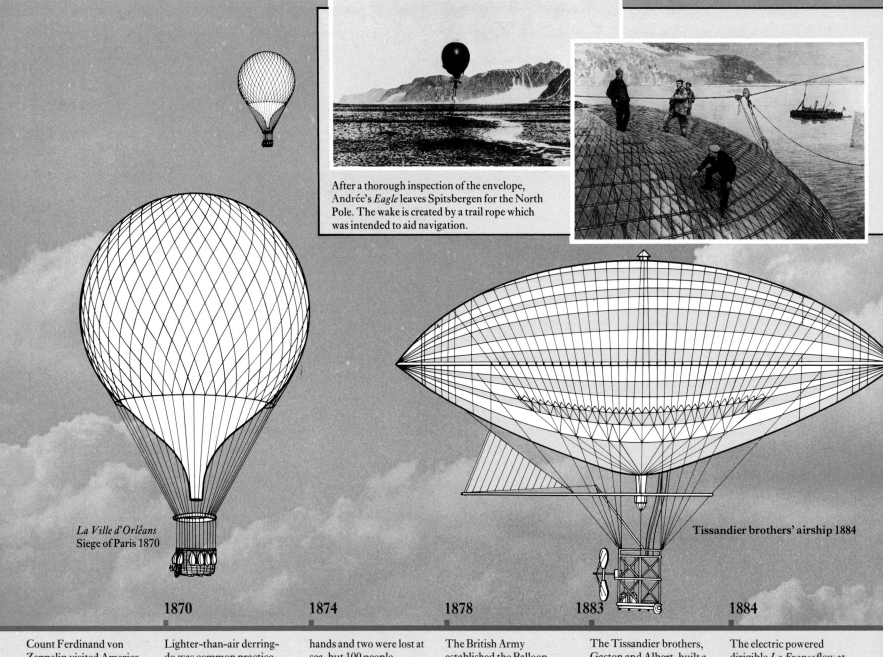

After a thorough inspection of the envelope, Andrée's *Eagle* leaves Spitsbergen for the North Pole. The wake is created by a trail rope which was intended to aid navigation.

La Ville d'Orléans
Siege of Paris 1870

Tissandier brothers' airship 1884

1870

1874

1878

1883

1884

Count Ferdinand von Zeppelin visited America to investigate the progress of the Civil War. Piloted by John Steiner, the count was flown in a balloon to a height of 700 ft.
An American named Andrews designed the first multi-hulled balloon, *Aereon*, which was also the first dirigible, although unpowered, to fly in America.

Lighter-than-air derring-do was common practice during the siege of Paris. The French, who were surrounded by Prusso – German forces, adapted balloons to carry refugees and mail. Between September 1870 and January 1871, 62 balloons were built in Paris. Of these six fell into enemy

hands and two were lost at sea, but 100 people escaped, along with over $2\frac{1}{2}$ million letters.

Félix du Temple's dream of heavier-than-air flight was realized when his full-sized plane took off from a ramp with a man aboard.

The British Army established the Balloon Equipment Store under Captains Lee and Templer. The first balloon was the 10,000 cu ft *Pioneer* which flew on August 23.

The Tissandier brothers, Gaston and Albert, built a 92 ft-long dirigible powered by a 1·5 hp motor. The airship flew twice and was abandoned in 1884.

The electric powered dirigible *La France* flew at over 14 mph. This airship demonstrated that it was possible to steer a course but *La France* only flew five times. Its problem was lack of power. It was *La France* which inspired Zeppelin to promote military airships in Germany.

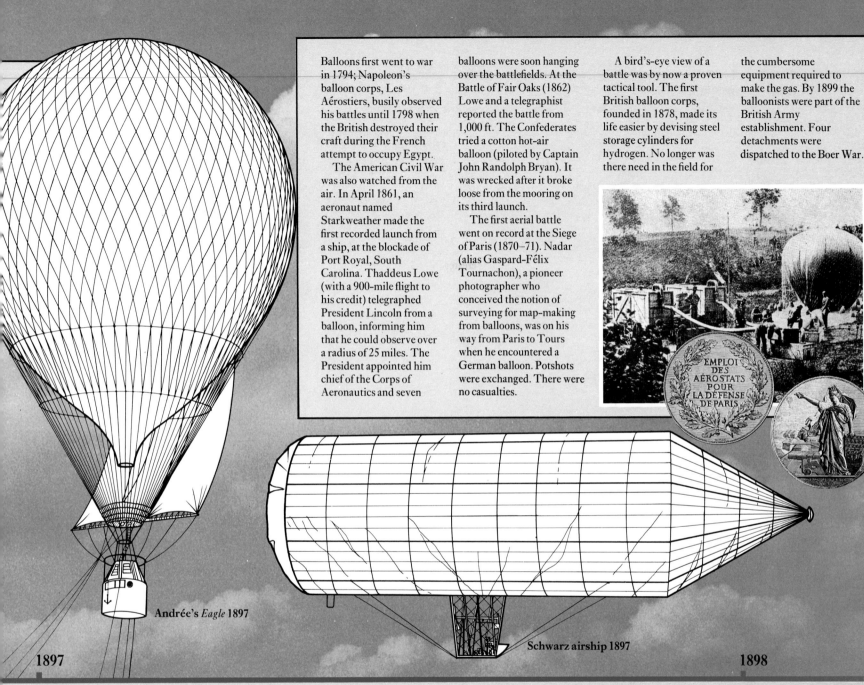

Balloons first went to war in 1794; Napoleon's balloon corps, Les Aérostiers, busily observed his battles until 1798 when the British destroyed their craft during the French attempt to occupy Egypt.

The American Civil War was also watched from the air. In April 1861, an aeronaut named Starkweather made the first recorded launch from a ship, at the blockade of Port Royal, South Carolina. Thaddeus Lowe (with a 900-mile flight to his credit) telegraphed President Lincoln from a balloon, informing him that he could observe over a radius of 25 miles. The President appointed him chief of the Corps of Aeronautics and seven balloons were soon hanging over the battlefields. At the Battle of Fair Oaks (1862) Lowe and a telegraphist reported the battle from 1,000 ft. The Confederates tried a cotton hot-air balloon (piloted by Captain John Randolph Bryan). It was wrecked after it broke loose from the mooring on its third launch.

The first aerial battle went on record at the Siege of Paris (1870–71). Nadar (alias Gaspard–Félix Tournachon), a pioneer photographer who conceived the notion of surveying for map-making from balloons, was on his way from Paris to Tours when he encountered a German balloon. Potshots were exchanged. There were no casualties.

A bird's-eye view of a battle was by now a proven tactical tool. The first British balloon corps, founded in 1878, made its life easier by devising steel storage cylinders for hydrogen. No longer was there need in the field for the cumbersome equipment required to make the gas. By 1899 the balloonists were part of the British Army establishment. Four detachments were dispatched to the Boer War.

Andrée's *Eagle* 1897

Schwarz airship 1897

1897

The Swedish aeronaut Salomon Andrée made an ill-advised attempt to reach the North Pole by balloon. Accompanied by two scientists in the balloon *Eagle*, he took off in July 1897. Apart from a message sent on the third day by carrier pigeon, there was no news and the ending of the voyage remained a mystery for 33 years, until the remains of the adventurers were discovered by Norwegian explorers.

Pibals were small unmanned balloons used to monitor the upper winds. Tracked by telescope until bursting at high altitude, they were the forerunners of the present day radio sonde and GHOST balloons.

The Schwarz rigid airship might have been more successful if its inventor, an Austrian engineer, had lived to finish his project. His wife brought it to completion. The rigid airship had a volume of 130,600 cu ft, and a a pointed nose cone like that of a rocket. The unique cylindrical structure was made entirely of aluminium. The ship was launched on a windy day and crashed within seconds of take-off.

1898

Inventors all over the world took advantage of the new internal combustion engine in attempts to fly. The first flight under such power was made by Santos-Dumont in Paris.

1899

British military balloons were used as observation platforms in South Africa during the Boer War. The balloons were filled with 13,000 cu ft of hydrogen.

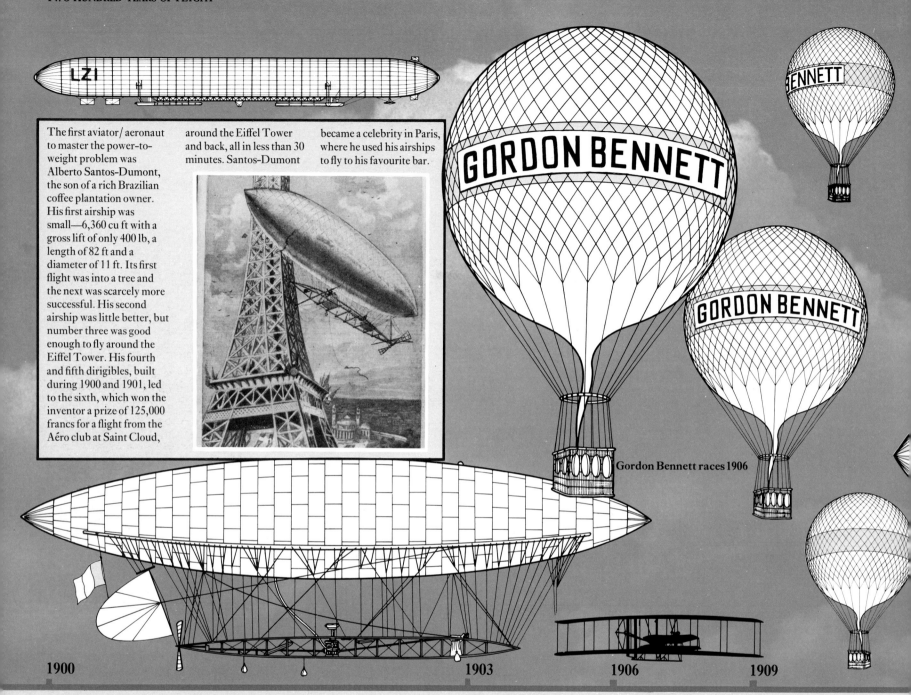

The first aviator/aeronaut to master the power-to-weight problem was Alberto Santos-Dumont, the son of a rich Brazilian coffee plantation owner. His first airship was small—6,360 cu ft with a gross lift of only 400 lb, a length of 82 ft and a diameter of 11 ft. Its first flight was into a tree and the next was scarcely more successful. His second airship was little better, but number three was good enough to fly around the Eiffel Tower. His fourth and fifth dirigibles, built during 1900 and 1901, led to the sixth, which won the inventor a prize of 125,000 francs for a flight from the Aéro club at Saint Cloud, around the Eiffel Tower and back, all in less than 30 minutes. Santos-Dumont became a celebrity in Paris, where he used his airships to fly to his favourite bar.

Gordon Bennett races 1906

1900

1903

1906

1909

Count Ferdinand von Zeppelin retired from the Prussian Army in 1891 and formed the 'Company for the Promotion of Airships'. Rigid airships were his invention. The first, LZ1, was begun in 1896, in a floating shed on Lake Constance, bordering Switzerland and Germany. A light zinc-aluminium alloy frame, covered in doped cloth, contained separate gas cells. The giant machine (420 ft long, 39 ft in diameter, with a volume of 399,054 cu ft) was ludicrously underpowered; the two Daimler engines provided less than 30 hp. But it flew—at 8 pm on July 2, 1900.

On December 17, 1903, Orville Wright flew a glider he had built with his brother, powered by an engine he designed himself, for 12 seconds. It was the first true flight of a heavier-than-air craft. Towards the end of the same day, his brother Wilbur flew *Flyer One* 852 ft in 59 seconds.

Gordon Bennett, the American newspaper proprietor gave his name and some of his money to ballooning's first international race. On September 30, 1906, 250,000 spectators watched 16 balloons lift off from Paris. The winner, F. P. Lahm, landed in Yorkshire, England, after a 22-hour flight.

By 1909 the Zeppelin-built airships were sufficiently reliable and controllable to give rise to the idea of a commercial 'airline', independent of government and military finance. DELAG (as Zeppelin's joint venture with the Hamburg–America Steamship Company was called) operated daily flights, so

Oars, paddles and flapping wings had all been tried by early balloonists as means of lessening their dependency on the vagaries of the wind. But it was 1837 before Sir George Cayley produced the first deisgn, never built, for a craft that was truly 'dirigible' or capable of being guided. Its cigar-shaped envelope was more streamlined than the traditional sphere, with steam-driven propellers for propulsion and a rudimentary rudder for steering.

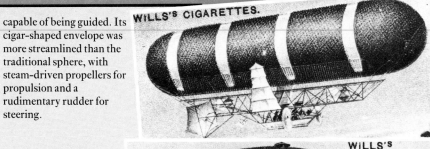

WILLS'S CIGARETTES.

WILLS'S CIGARETTES.

FIRST SUCCESSFUL DIRIGIBLE.

ATTERRISSAGE DU BALLON DIRIGEABLE LE «JAUNE» A LA GALERIE DES MACHINES

Willows' *City of Cardiff* 1909

ET WILLOWS Nº3.

1910

America 1910

that in Germany city after city caught 'airship fever'.

More observation jaunts than scheduled services, the flights none the less showed the potential of the massive airships (LZ5 flew 750 miles in 39 hours in 1909). DELAG was growing strongly when World War I put a stop to its relaxed excursions.

E. T. Willows was the British equivalent of Santos-Dumont, and was popularly known as the father of British airships. His story is a wretched one. Bad luck and lack of finance accompanied him throughout his career until his death in a spherical balloon in 1926. His major success was the Willows II also known as *City of Cardiff*, an airship of 21,000 cu ft with a length of 86 ft, which was flown from London to Cardiff. A novel feature was the use of swivelling propellers, enabling the pilot to direct the airship up and down.

In July 1909 Louis Blériot became the first pilot to cross the English Channel in a powered aircraft. The $23\frac{1}{2}$-mile flight lasted $36\frac{1}{2}$ minutes.

The airship *America*, brainchild of the American journalist and explorer Walter Wellman made three unsuccessful attempts to reach the North Pole (1907–09), before exploding on the ice. Undaunted, Wellman pointed its successor and namesake across the Atlantic in 1910. The 228-ft airship set off on October 15, from Atlantic City, New Jersey, with six men and a stowaway kitten on board. One engine soon failed, leaving the other overworked. Just over 1,000 miles out, a British ship picked the crew out of the ocean.

America's place in history is derived from the fact that it sent the world's first air-to-sea radio message: 'Come to fetch that damn cat.'

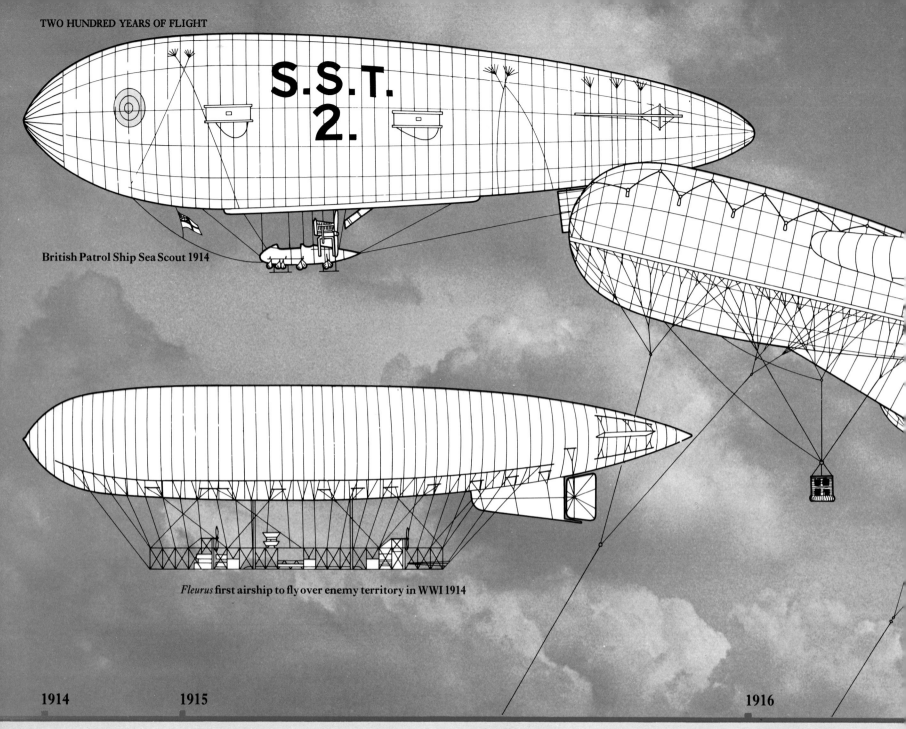

British Patrol Ship Sea Scout 1914

Fleurus first airship to fly over enemy territory in WWI 1914

1914

1915

1916

The first bombing of Britain from the air had little effect. The early Zeppelin raids were in the north of England, from Barrow in the west to the Humber.

The French, first to use observation balloons in 1794, were also the first to disband their balloon corps, in 1912. Early in World War I, however, following the successful use of observation balloons by the German forces, the French were forced to readopt these clumsy vessels.

Captain Albert Caquot developed a new type of self-stabilizing, finned blimp which could remain in the air indefinitely. This was loosely based on the German Drachen, or kite-balloon, which combined the principles of both balloons and kites.

Built in a range of sizes from 26,000 – 35,000 cu ft, the kite-balloons were used for observing troop movements and directing gunfire to such good effect that they became prime targets for fighter pilots. As the balloons were filled with hydrogen they were extremely vulnerable to tracer bullets. If attacked by aircraft they could be hauled down by powerful winches at 1,500 fpm.

After making the first successful attack on a German airship—SLII, a Schütte-Lanz rigid type—fighter pilot Leefe Robinson was awarded the Victoria Cross.

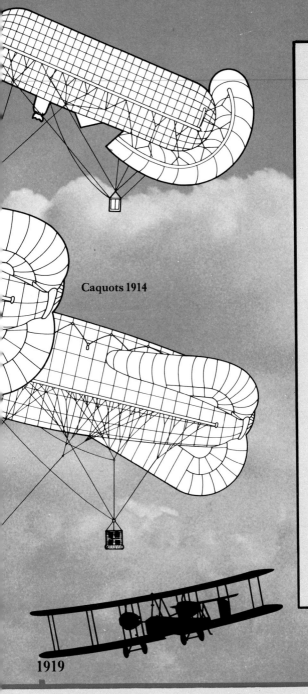

Caquots 1914

1919

The outbreak of war found the Germans surprisingly ill-equipped for aerial warfare; the first air attack on Britain did not take place until January 19/20, 1915. But soon Zeppelins became a menace to the citizens of England's coastal regions, dropping bombs haphazardly and inflicting both psychological and physical damage. The early ships contained up to 800,000 cu ft of hydrogen and could fly at 9,000 ft, with a top speed of 53 mph and a range of 700 miles. By May 1915 the volume was increased to 1,126,500 cu ft. The top speed was now 59 mph, the ceiling 12,800 ft and the range doubled. Although there were rapid advances in Zeppelin's designs the poor quality of navigational equipment at the time meant that a lot of bomb tonnage was dropped on non-strategic sites.

In four years the Zeppelins had developed from primitive, slow craft with exposed crew quarters, into large, sleek ships capable of spending days in the skies and maintaining the crews in reasonable comfort. As the war drew to a close the later machines had a volume of over 2 million cu ft, a speed of 78 mph, an operational ceiling of 23,000 ft and a cruising range of 3,730 miles. These airships were quite capable of crossing the Atlantic under favourable conditions.

Perhaps the best-known heroic episode of the Zeppelin at war was the epic flight of LZ 104 (L 59). In November 1917 the airship, under the command of Ludwig Bockholt, set out carrying 16 tons of armaments, stores and mail to relieve German troops in East Africa.

Unknown to the crew, Germany's African forces surrendered as the airship took off. Trouble with the radio transmitter, and local electric storms, kept the crew unaware of the pointless nature of their flight. They were over Africa by the time the recall message was heard. The weary crew brought the ship back, unharmed, to their base in Bulgaria, having flown 4,040 miles in 95 hours.

During the course of the war, over 115 Zeppelins were built and 22 out of 50 trained crews died in action or as the result of accidents. On Germany's surrender in 1918, the Allies' reparation terms included the closing of many German aircraft factories. An initial order for the destruction of the Zeppelin plant was reversed, but the company was required to hand over its existing airships and to build several new models for the Allies. To ensure the company's survival, Dr. Hugo Eckener, Count Zeppelin's successor, formed a business partnership with the Goodyear Tire & Rubber Company of America.

In June 1919 Alcock and Brown won the £10,000 *Daily Mail* prize for the first men to cross the Atlantic by air in an uninterrupted flight. Their aircraft, a Vickers Vimy, took off from Newfoundland, flew 1,936 miles in 16 hours 27 minutes and crashed into an Irish bog, at the absolute limit of its range. The flight was bedevilled by bad weather and mechanical problems, and Brown was frequently obliged to climb on to the wings to hack off fast-forming ice.

PUBLIC WARNING

The public are advised to familiarise themselves with the appearance of British and German Airships and Aeroplanes, so that they may not be alarmed by British aircraft, and may take shelter if German aircraft appear. **Should hostile aircraft be seen**, take shelter immediately in the nearest available house, preferably in the basement, and remain there until the aircraft have left the vicinity: do not stand about in crowds **and do not touch unexploded bombs**.

In the event of HOSTILE aircraft being seen in country districts, the nearest Naval, Military or Police Authorities should, if possible, be advised immediately by Telephone of the TIME OF APPEARANCE, the DIRECTION OF FLIGHT, and whether the aircraft is an Airship or an Aeroplane.

GERMAN AIRSHIPS

BRITISH AIRSHIPS

AEROPLANES

AEROPLANES

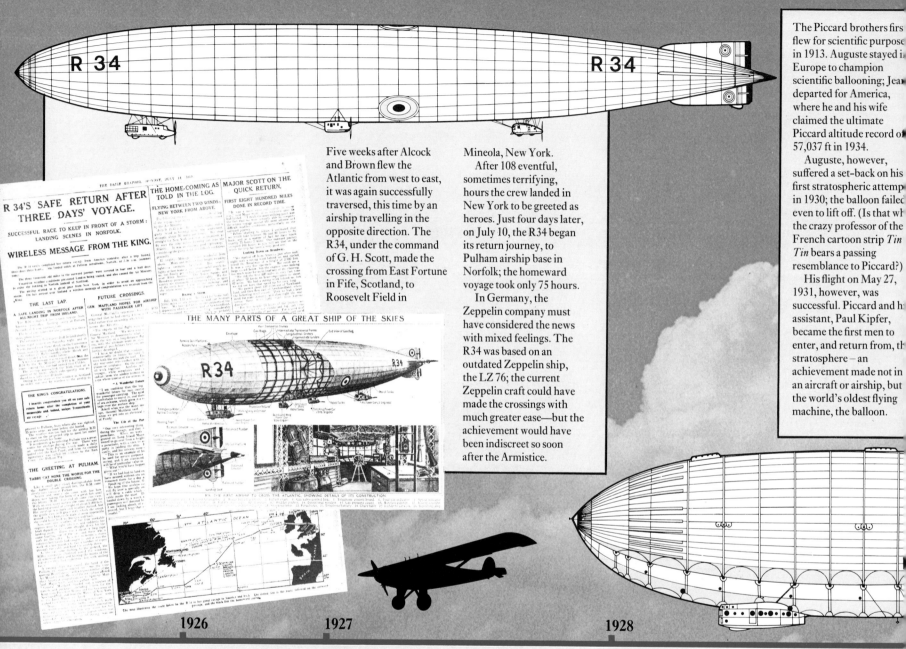

Five weeks after Alcock and Brown flew the Atlantic from west to east, it was again successfully traversed, this time by an airship travelling in the opposite direction. The R34, under the command of G. H. Scott, made the crossing from East Fortune in Fife, Scotland, to Roosevelt Field in Mineola, New York.

After 108 eventful, sometimes terrifying, hours the crew landed in New York to be greeted as heroes. Just four days later, on July 10, the R34 began its return journey, to Pulham airship base in Norfolk; the homeward voyage took only 75 hours.

In Germany, the Zeppelin company must have considered the news with mixed feelings. The R34 was based on an outdated Zeppelin ship, the LZ 76; the current Zeppelin craft could have made the crossings with much greater ease—but the achievement would have been indiscreet so soon after the Armistice.

The Piccard brothers firs[t] flew for scientific purpose[s] in 1913. Auguste stayed i[n] Europe to champion scientific ballooning; Jea[n] departed for America, where he and his wife claimed the ultimate Piccard altitude record o[f] 57,037 ft in 1934.

Auguste, however, suffered a set-back on his first stratospheric attemp[t] in 1930; the balloon faile[d] even to lift off. (Is that wh[y] the crazy professor of the French cartoon strip *Tin Tin* bears a passing resemblance to Piccard?)

His flight on May 27, 1931, however, was successful. Piccard and h[is] assistant, Paul Kipfer, became the first men to enter, and return from, th[e] stratosphere – an achievement made not in an aircraft or airship, but the world's oldest flying machine, the balloon.

1926

Roald Amundsen, the first man to reach the South Pole, was aboard the first airship to cross the North Pole in 1926. The *Norge* (N1) was built and piloted by Umberto Nobile. It was while searching for Nobile's second, ill-fated, Arctic expedition, two years later, that Amundsen met his death in a plane crash.

1927

The transatlantic flight of Charles A. Lindbergh in the *Spirit of St Louis* in May was the first-ever solo crossing of the Atlantic, a milestone in aviation history. Taking off from Roosevelt Field in Mineola he reached Le Bourget, Paris, 3,609 miles away, only 33 hours 39 minutes later. Lindbergh's solo flight won him undying fame.

US Army Captain Hawthorne C. Grey made the first stratospheric flights. His first attempt was discounted as he abandoned his balloon (incidentally establishing a long-standing free-fall parachute record). On his second flight he stayed with the balloon and established an altitude record of 42,470 ft but Grey was found dead in the gondola.

General Nobile's second polar expedition was in 1928 in the *Italia*, a small, semi-rigid airship which set off from King's Bay, Spitsbergen, with a crew of 16. The flight to the Pole was easy, but on the return journey increasing headwinds forced the *Italia* into the ice pack. After several weeks nine survivors were rescued, including Nobile.

1928

The brainchild of Dr. Hugo Eckener, who spent six years raising funds for her construction, *Graf Zeppelin* took to the skies on July 8, 1928, the ninetieth anniversary of the count's birth.

The *Graf*, a prophetic symbol of the emerging new Germany, achieved the first circumnavigation of the world in 1929, during which she travelled

In a pressurized spherical, aluminium gondola (based on the design of a beer-brewing tank) Piccard rose to 51,793 ft. To control the temperature in the gondola Piccard had painted it half black and half white, and installed a motor that could turn it so that either the reflective white or heat-absorbent black side could be turned to face the sun. The motor refused to work, however, and with the black side facing sunwards it appeared quite probable, as the temperature passed 100°F, that the two men would literally be cooked alive. Condensation on the cold side of the gondola saved them.

After a hair-raising descent the balloon pitched into the snow half-way up a glacier in the Italian Alps. Piccard and Kipfer were saved but it was nearly a year before the gondola could be recovered.

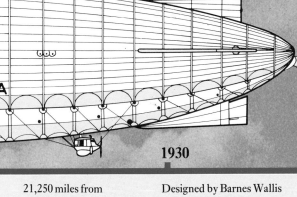

1930   **1933**   **1935**

21,250 miles from Lakehurst via Friedrichshafen (where Zeppelin built his first airships) Tokyo, and Los Angeles, back to Lakehurst—1,000 miles a day for 21 days, carrying 20 passengers in the luxury of an ocean liner. In the same year, the Zeppelin company began to plan the first-ever scheduled North Atlantic crossings.

Designed by Barnes Wallis and built by Vickers to compete with the government-backed R101, the R100, 'the Capitalist Airship', made a safe, easy crossing to Canada and back in 1930. With an exceptionally light yet strong hull structure, she was the most advanced airship of her time.

In the period 1933–35 the Americans and the Russians engaged in a preview of their later space race. At the time the stratosphere provided the challenge and balloons were the vehicles.

On November 20–21, 1933, Maj. C. L. Fordney and Lt. Cdr. T. G. W. Settle piloted a Goodyear-made helium-filled strato-balloon to 54,675 ft. In January 1934 the Soviet balloon *Ossoaviaklium* reached the incredible altitude of 72,178 ft. But the gondola tore loose on the descent and the crew, unable to force open the gondola hatch to jump out, were killed.

On June 28, 1934, W. E. Kepner, A. W. Stevens and O. A. Anderson in *Explorer I* reached 60,000 ft over Nebraska. On the descent the envelope developed a horizontal tear and the balloon plunged downwards. The crew managed to bail out, one by one, as the balloon fabric disintegrated above them, and parachute to safety.

Finally on November 11, 1935, the Russians were bettered, as Stevens and Anderson reached a height of 74,185 ft in the giant 3,700,000 cu ft *Explorer II*, a record which remained unbroken for 21 years.

They launched from Strato-Bowl in South Dakota, later to be the scene of the first successful modern hot-air balloon flight.

The *Hindenburg*, nearer the size of an airport than an aircraft, was by far the largest flying machine ever built. It was built to provide a regular service between Germany and New York while the *Graf Zeppelin*, half the volume, made her stately way to Brazil.

These were the first transatlantic air services. The *Hindenburg*'s enormity was largely based upon the expectation that she would be filled with non-flammable helium (still fresh were memories of the R101 disaster in which 48 people had perished amid 5 million cubic feet of flaming hydrogen). While safer than hydrogen, helium is a less effective lifting agent and so a greater volume is required. In the 1930s helium was a rare commodity, over which the USA had an effective monopoly. In the event, for political reasons, the helium was not forthcoming, and when the *Hindenburg* first flew on March 4, 1936, hydrogen was the lifting gas.

At first all went well. The *Hindenburg* flew a total of 56 flights carrying 2,656 passengers in the greatest of luxury and comfort. Her sister ship *Graf Zeppelin* had 650 successful flights to her credit, had flown a million kilometres and carried over 18,000 passengers. At this point the Zeppelin company could proudly claim that no passenger had ever been killed or injured on one of their airships.

On May 4, 1937, the *Hindenburg* left Frankfurt Rhein-Main airport on her first scheduled flight to Lakehurst, New Jersey, under the experienced command of Captain Max Pruss. The flight across the Atlantic was uneventful, and at 3.30 pm on May 6 the huge ship flew gracefully over the Empire State Building *en route* for Lakehurst. Local electric storms delayed her final approach, and she eventually eased towards the mooring mast 13 hours behind schedule. The hum of her five engines rose to a roar as at maximum pitch she reversed engines and slowed to a halt. The mooring ropes went down to the engines on the circular track around the mast. Aboard the ship all was normal and the radio operator was in contact with the distant *Graf Zeppelin* on her way back from Rio far across the southern Atlantic.

And then, suddenly, flames burst out of the rear of the hull and the airship, consumed by fire, fell vertically 60 feet to the ground. To horrified witnesses it seemed impossible that anybody could escape from the holocaust, but miraculously 62 out of 97 passengers aboard survived. Was it St. Elmo's fire or static electricity setting escaping gas alight? To this day the *Hindenburg* disaster remains the most mysterious of all airship accidents. One theory that has gained popularity is that of sabotage. Quite unwillingly the giant Zeppelin had become the victim of politics. Forced to carry the hated swastikas of Nazi Germany, it seems that the *Hindenburg* may well have been sabotaged, a combination of her very late arrival at Lakehurst and a delayed-action fuse causing an unintended and tragic loss of life.

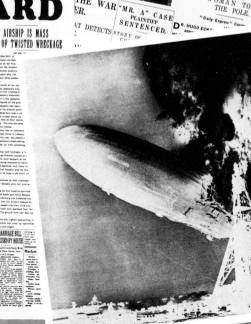

1936

Hindenburg, commissioned in March 1936, was assigned builder's number LZ 129 (Luftschiff Zeppelin 129). It was the 118th Zeppelin built. More than 10 miles of Duralumin, a light alloy of copper and aluminium, were used in the construction.

The swastikas painted on the tail fins caused ill feeling. There had been riots on the liner *Bremen* months earlier in protest against the Nazi regime. Shots were fired at the *Hindenburg* as she passed over America and after every voyage riggers checked the outer hull for bullet holes.

The outer skin was a strong cotton fabric, stretched and sewn to the framework, then doped with five coats of cellon, mixed with silver to reflect the heat. The inside of the top was painted red as protection against ultraviolet rays.

The engine pods were streamlined like eggs. Inside the pods 16-cylinder V-type Daimler-Benz diesels drove four-bladed wooden propellers, 20 ft in diameter. Between them, the four engines delivered 5,000 horsepower.

The crew dressed in specially designed one piece overalls, with no buttons to snag on the intricate internal wiring. Shoes had crêpe soles with canvas uppers; the eyes were reinforced with cloth, not metal, and even the metal bands at the end of the shoelaces were eliminated.

Vents on the top of the hull forced clean air through the ship to blow away traces of leaking gas.

Olympic symbols were applied to *Hindenburg* and *Graf Zeppelin* both of which flew over the 1936 Olympic Games in Berlin.

Passengers entered on B deck. An aisle ran forward to the bar, where a steward was on duty, night and day, guarding a double locked door which led to the smoking room—the only place on the *Hindenburg* where smoking was allowed.

Upstairs on A deck there was a library and a large lounge which contained a lightweight piano and a writing room. Behind the windows was the 130-ft promenade deck. Inboard of the port promenade was the restaurant, seating 80

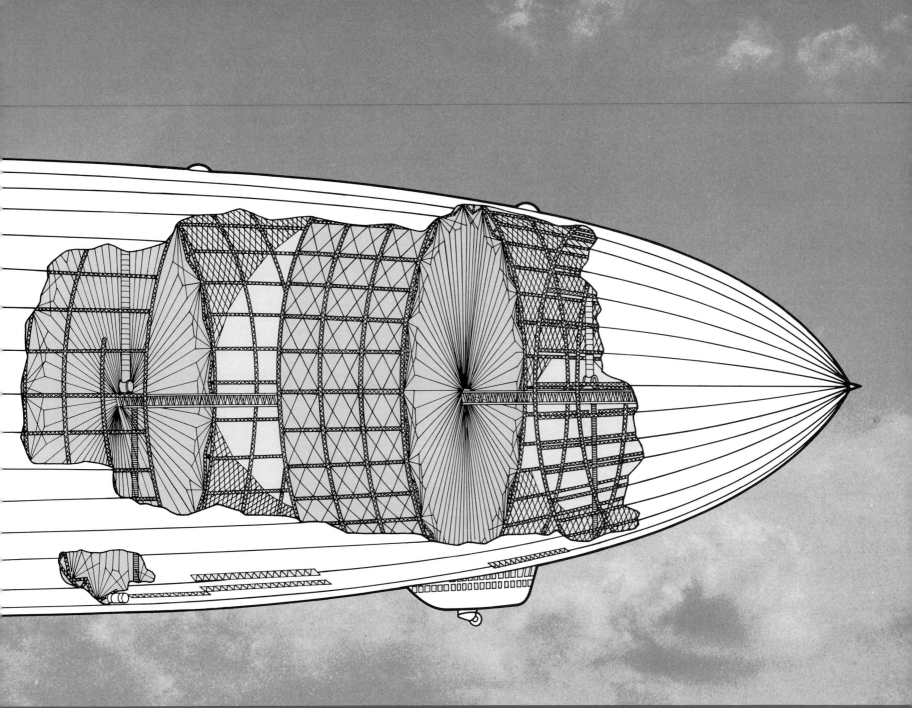

passengers. In the centre of A deck were 25 staterooms arranged side by side and running fore and aft. Each contained its own bathroom and sitting room. They were serviced by a team of 8 stewards and stewardesses.

Sixteen gas bags—one to each compartment—were made from cotton fabric, backed with chemically produced film. Each bag was held in place by a rope netting—the same method as on the first gas balloon.

When all 16 gas cells were inflated, they contained 7,100,000 cu ft of hydrogen—enough to lift a gross weight of 236 tons. With a full payload of 20 tons *Hindenburg* could cruise for over 8,000 miles, (or 6 days) at 80 mph. Accommodation for 72 passengers was on two decks inside the hull.

The command gondola was 28 ft long and 9 ft wide. A retractable landing wheel fitted into its base. Facing forward was the steering compartment, behind which were two large navigating rooms. Commands were signalled by mechanical telegraph and telephone or, in case of failure, by speaking tubes.

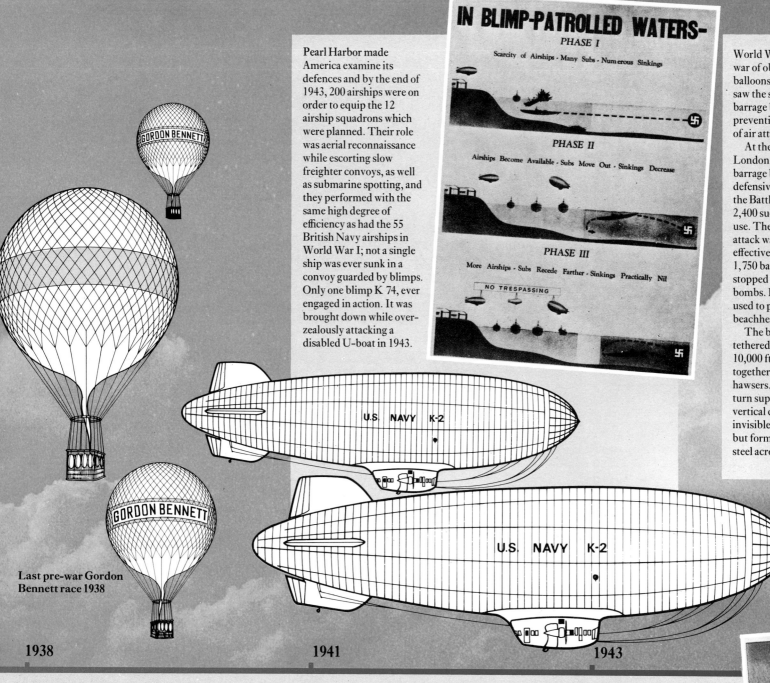

Pearl Harbor made America examine its defences and by the end of 1943, 200 airships were on order to equip the 12 airship squadrons which were planned. Their role was aerial reconnaissance while escorting slow freighter convoys, as well as submarine spotting, and they performed with the same high degree of efficiency as had the 55 British Navy airships in World War I; not a single ship was ever sunk in a convoy guarded by blimps. Only one blimp K 74, ever engaged in action. It was brought down while over-zealously attacking a disabled U-boat in 1943.

IN BLIMP-PATROLLED WATERS-

PHASE I

Scarcity of Airships · Many Subs · Numerous Sinkings

PHASE II

Airships Become Available · Subs Move Out · Sinkings Decrease

PHASE III

More Airships · Subs Recede Farther · Sinkings Practically Nil

NO TRESPASSING

World War I had been the war of observation balloons. World War II saw the successful use of barrage balloons in the prevention and disruption of air attacks.

At the outbreak of war, London already had 450 barrage balloons as a defensive screen. During the Battle of Britain over 2,400 such units were in use. The VI 'Doodle-bug' attack was reduced in its effectiveness by the use of 1,750 balloons which stopped 279 of the flying bombs. Finally they were used to protect the D-Day beachheads.

The balloons were tethered at heights of up to 10,000 ft and connected together by long steel hawsers. The hawsers in turn supported a mesh of vertical cables, virtually invisible to the naked eye, but forming a curtain of steel across the sky.

GORDON BENNETT

GORDON BENNETT

Last pre-war Gordon Bennett race 1938

U.S. NAVY K-2

U.S. NAVY K-2

1938

1941

1943

CHURCHMAN'S CIGARETTES

REPRESENTATION OF BALLO... BARRAGE FOR DEFENCE OF L...

Fu-Gos 1944

1944

Don Piccard 1947

1947

Balloons have been a part of the military scene since they were invented but World War II saw one of the most bizarre—and unsuccessful—uses ever devised.

The Japanese high command planned to demoralize the West Coast population of the USA by launching small hydrogen balloons, carrying loads of between 5–15 kg of incendiaries and explosives, designed to cause random havoc. Weather limitations were taken into account and the launchings were made while the east wind was prevailing, between October and March.

In all some 9,000 of the Fu-Gos were launched in the five-month period commencing November 1944. The scheme was hare-brained and only 285 balloons made recorded landfall on America. This seems a high percentage considering they followed random paths over the Pacific, where the shortest crossing was 6,000 miles, and the balloons ended up spread widely from Alaska to Mexico. Only six deaths and minimal damage occurred.

Don Piccard, son of Jean and Jeanette, made his first flight in 1933. After World War II he put one of the few Fu-Gos that reached the USA to more practical use and made what was probably the first post-war free flight in 1947.

The hot-air revival

The golden age of ballooning ended abruptly in 1939, and for six years the skies of Europe echoed to the roar of more deadly flying machines. Ironically, it was to be the continuation of hostilities, in the Cold War of the 50s, that revived interest in ballooning, and also provided the technological impetus for the rebirth of the hot-air balloon.

In the austere years after the war there were few balloons in non-military use and those which did exist were flown only occasionally, due to the difficulty of obtaining hydrogen. In post-war Europe those still practising the art of aerostation included the inveterate French balloonist Dollfus and Dolder from Switzerland. Don Piccard added to his family's ballooning achievements by making the first post-war American flight in 1947. But balloon sport was non-existent and the prospects were gloomy. Ballooning is a light-hearted activity which has to be supported by a comfortable standard of living; and hydrogen was an expensive commodity.

During this period a young American named Ed Yost was in Europe, working for the General Mills company on high altitude gas balloons for scientific and probably espionage projects. Yost's company was sub-contracted by Radio Free Europe to distribute propaganda leaflets behind the Iron Curtain from bases in West Germany. Yost designed and built the propaganda balloons, each of which lifted off from the ashes of the war-ravaged country like the mythical Phoenix. It was this political use of balloons which led, indirectly, to the revival of hot-air ballooning.

The hot-air method of aerostation had lost favour in the early years due to the lack of suitable means of generating and containing the hot air. Yost was the first person to apply modern technology to the eighteenth-century invention.

His hydrogen-filled leaflet balloons were made of polythene, a General Mills product, which was heat-welded to shape. The early models had a payload of 4 lb of leaflets and a quantity of dry-ice for automatic ballasting. In the course of his experiments, Yost attached a plumber's blowtorch to an 8,000 cu ft polythene envelope and, in 1953, he flew it. The first of a new generation of hot-air balloons had left the ground.

Within two days of his first flight, Yost had a balloon of twice the volume in the air, capable of lifting its own fuel and 40 lb of payload, including the three blowtorches which powered it. Within weeks Yost's team had produced a 27,000 cu ft model, 39 ft in diameter, which could easily lift a man.

As with many other high-technology spin-offs, hot-air ballooning would have developed more slowly if it had not had a military potential. The US Navy thought they could make use of man-carrying balloons and, when Yost applied to the Office of Naval Research (ONR) for a grant to further his studies, his research programme was funded to the tune of $47,000.

Yost remembers that in those days five flights was the maximum life span of an envelope; so much thought was given to the selection of suitable coating for the nylon envelope cloth. The team was also researching into new and improved burners, trying to overcome the problems of pressurizing gasoline to lift it to the burner and beginning to realize the advantages of gases, such as propane, which are bottled under pressure.

In 1956 Yost and three partners formed Raven Industries to construct high altitude balloons and to continue research into man-carrying hot-air balloons. Raven obtained a further grant from the ONR for the development of a two-man balloon, which the US Navy intended to use as a trainer for airship pilots. (The US Navy operated blimps into the early 1960s as a part of the early warning and coastal surveillance system).

Four more years of research into subjects such as temperature profiles and burner performance produced the prototype 'modern' hot-air balloon. The 30,000 cu ft envelope, 40 ft in diameter, was constructed of a polyurethane-coated nylon and the burner was propane-powered. The first man-carrying free flight took place at Bruning, Nebraska, on October 10, 1960, the official birth date of the modern hot-air balloon.

The flight was short-lived because lack of burner power convinced Yost that the craft was unsafe. What had happened was that in trying to

Charles Dollfus, gas balloonist from another era

Ed Yost, hot air in the Cold War

draw off sufficient vapour to fuel the burner, he was causing the system to freeze up, with burner failure inevitably resulting.

One month later, Yost had rectified the problem by constructing a dip-tube to draw off liquid propane and then vaporizing the liquid in the flame-heated coil. He had built a crude prototype of the modern burner. It took him to a height of 9,300 ft above Strato-Bowl, South Dakota. It is interesting to note that Yost rose to about the same height as J.A.C. Charles had on his second flight back in 1783. Ballooning had obviously been reborn.

In pioneering the hot-air revival, Yost took risks which an educated present-day pilot would not. His prototype machine had an explosive rip panel and only a single needle valve to control the flow of propane to the burner; a minor failure in either system would have proved disastrous. Had the rip been opened inadvertently he would have come down fast—as he would if the burner had failed. Neither system was fail-safe and there were no back-up facilities to use in the event of failure.

Later that year Yost teamed up with Don Piccard, already an experienced gas balloon pilot, to promote hot-air ballooning as a popular sport. Piccard and Yost travelled to Britain in 1963 to exhibit their latest Raven product, a 60,000 cu ft balloon, 50 ft in diameter. At the old airship sheds in Cardington they met Anthony Smith, the British balloonist and writer, who helped them arrange a cross-channel flight to demonstrate the Raven's capabilities.

In the last week of March, Yost and Piccard made the first ever crossing of the English Channel by hot-air balloon. They were airborne for 3 hours 17 minutes, flying mainly at or above 13,000 ft, and the balloon, immediately christened *Channel Champ*, deposited the two men safely in France, close to the Belgium border.

The two aeronauts were lucky to make it since

the wind was far from suitable, but as Yost says, 'We had to succeed because our only way of returning to America was in free seats on a military plane leaving Paris the next day.'

Yost pioneered, Piccard promoted. Very soon Piccard's enthusiasm and his flair for publicity were attracting customers from the ranks of adventure sportsmen. The first hot-air balloons sold in Britain, France, Sweden, Denmark and South Africa bore the logo of Piccard's own company.

Yost and Piccard reintroduced hot-air ballooning to Europe but there was another American who was also influential in early balloon development. Tracy Barnes, a physics

Early Raven balloons flying in America

student from the University of Minnesota, had become interested in the recreational potential of hot-air ballooning, inspired by his friend Bill Hutch, a member of the Raven development team.

In 1961 Barnes built himself a balloon which he flew to 8,000 ft. Five years later he made the first transamerican hot-air flight. His development work, on parachute rip systems and more effective burners and baskets, brought modern ballooning into its next phase. In 1963 the growing sport was able to sustain the first US national championships, and by the mid-1960s there were three manufacturers: the dominant Raven, and Piccard and Barnes.

A Piccard balloon (*Red Dragon*, owned by Leslie Goldsmith) was one of the three which launched the sport in Britain—at Dunstable Gliding Club in August 1966, the year the British Balloon and Airship Club was founded. The others were a Montgolfier replica, built by apprentices at the Hawker Siddeley aircraft factory; and a 64,000 cu ft polythene balloon called the MK 6 Smithill which actually made a man-carrying flight.

Red Dragon launched the sport in Britain

The Smithill ended its brief voyage in power lines but the pilot escaped with the satisfaction of piloting the first flight of a British-built hot-air balloon.

The following winter a more conventional machine was being designed by Malcolm Brighton and Anthony Smith, the two most experienced balloonists in Britain. Built by a firm of parachute manufacturers in Suffolk, *Bristol Belle* tore itself apart on its first inflation in June 1967, due to the high envelope stresses inherent in the design. Don Cameron then made the first of his many contributions to ballooning when he took the envelope to another parachute manufacturer, RFD GQ, who remade it with horizontal load tapes to stop it tearing.

The MK 6 Smithill heading for the power lines

At this time *Bristol Belle*, owned and operated by the newly formed Hot Air Group, was the only British-built balloon flying. The inspiration to build it had come when Anthony Smith flew a Raven Vulcoon in America. He and Brighton had been more concerned with building gas balloons and airships and *Bristol Belle* was their only hot-air craft.

Most of the British balloon customers were now buying Piccards. *Red Dragon* was followed by *London Pride*, *Zumikon* and others. In the

Bristol Belle, with and without skirt

autumn of 1968, Cameron and Goldsmith, along with two others, founded Omega and British production balloons began to appear. Public interest in ballooning was stimulated by a big sponsored international meet at Dunstable in 1971 and by the Nimble Bread advertising campaign.

Omega split into Cameron Balloons and Western Balloons. Cameron delivered *Flaming Pearl*, an 84,000 cu ft balloon, in April 1970 and gave it c/n (construction number) 11, thus effectively continuing the numbering of the old Omega series. (Omega's last balloon, c/n 10, was *Nimble Two*). Western's first balloon, *Fiery Queen*, also 84,000 cu ft, was delivered to the London Balloon Club in July 1970.

Thunder Balloons was founded in 1972, when I teamed up with Tom Donnelly and Kenneth Simmonds to produce the first Thunder—as much out of dismay at the slow delivery on production balloons as from a desire to build to our own design. The 12-gore AX7 (77,000 cu ft) balloon, in the patriotic design of a Union Jack, made its maiden flight in January 1973 at the first British Icicle Meet. We took *Jumpin' Jack* to the USA for the first world championship that year and received our first customer order from a citizen of Albuquerque. This brought the total number of British manufacturers to three, but they were all some seven years behind the Americans.

In the early 1970s the only manufacturers of note outside Britain and America were in France. Montgolfier Moderne was started by Robbie Noirclerc, who returned from the 1973 world championships determined to revive the French dominance of ballooning; and Maurice Chaize, a sailmaker, occasionally builds hot-air balloons at his Lyon factory.

As the industry expanded in the 1970s Barnes' output increased to equal Raven's as top American manufacturer. Ed Yost sold his interest in Raven in 1972 to concentrate on building gas balloons. In 1976 he attempted a transatlantic crossing but it was another balloon of his manufacture, *Double Eagle II*, which finally succeeded in 1978.

Piccard continued to flourish in America as did Stokes, a builder of specialist custom balloons such as pressurized airships and advertising blimps. Small manufacturers like Adams and Avian started producing balloons in the popular classes. In the USA, where a small hot-air balloon costs no more than a big motorcycle, manufacturers have no trouble finding customers.

In Europe, Cameron remained the dominant manufacturer. Western faded away and Thunder grew throughout the 1970s as makers of high quality balloons. In France, Montgolfier Moderne flowered brilliantly, but briefly; they are now agents for Thunder. Chaize continues to build a small number of balloons in Lyon.

The ever-increasing demand for hot-air balloons led three Swedish aeronauts to found Colt in Britain in 1977. They specialize in ingeniously shaped advertising balloons.

London Pride, an American balloon for a British pilot

An early export for the British balloon business—with burner by Malcolm Brighton

The high-tech generation

Balloons are massive. A 64,000 cu ft envelope occupies as much space as a 40-ft cube—equivalent to the capacity of twenty-five 40-ft truck trailers, enclosed in 1,000 sq yds of material. To obtain lift an aerostat must displace several tons of air.

Most countries require that balloon manufacturers submit their products for theoretical and practical approval. In the USA the controlling body is the Federal Aviation Authority (FAA); in Britain it is the Civil Aviation Authority (CAA). The balloon types are issued with a certificate of airworthiness and each craft is submitted to a physical inspection annually, or after every 100 hours of flying, whichever is more frequent. On average a balloon will provide between 300 and 400 hours of safe flying before fabric weakness is detected.

Like any other aircraft, balloons must be registered in the country of origin. In the USA the registration number begins with the letter N—followed by a series of numbers and letters.

In Britain the prefix is always G—followed by four letters which are allocated in strict rotation. This leads to some competition in getting the meaningful sequences, like G-BAIR, G-HOST, G-ZUMP (owned by an estate agent); or the American N38AC, which records the bust size in inches before the initials of the owner's wife.

Hot air expands the envelope to the size of a house.

Hoover balloon has an appropriate registration number.

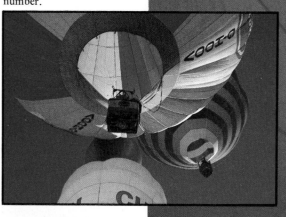

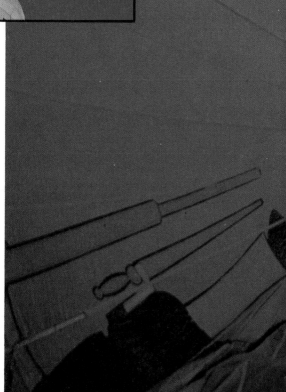

Government inspectors making pre-delivery checks on an envelope.

A pilot packs 1,000 sq yds of envelope into a 3ft cube.

Hot-air balloons are bigger than gas balloons because even heated air is much denser than hydrogen or helium, so more of it is needed to lift off. Typically a gas balloon (hydrogen) will derive about 60 lb of lift per 1,000 cu ft whereas a hot-air model will develop only 17–20 lb per 1,000 cu ft (at 100–120°C).

Thus a 77,000 cu ft balloon will lift: 77 x 17 = 1,309 lb gross lift. Assuming the weights are:

Envelope	– 160 lb
Basket and burner	– 150 lb
4 gas tanks	– 290 lb
Total	– 600 lb

Net lift: 1,309–600 = 709 lb

The average person weighs 170 lb and therefore a standard '77' operating in standard atmospheric conditions will lift 709/170 = 4·17 people – or three passengers, one pilot and equipment.

Type	Max Size (in cu ft)	Capacity (crew)
AX2	12,000	1
AX3	20,000	1
AX4	31,000	1
AX5	42,000	2
AX6	56,000	2/3
AX7	77,000	3/4
AX8	105,000	5/6
AX9	140,000	8
AX10	Unlimited	–

Colt – 'A' series
AX6 – AX8
Features a parachute rip and is similar in form to the Thunder on which it is modelled. The basket is wicker and the Colt burner has particularly efficient burning characteristics.

Thunder Bolt AX5 – AX7
A light, eight-gore model offered in a range of sizes in direct competition with the Cameron Viva. It has a distinctive tear-drop shape and features the Thunder parachute plug.

Raven S-55A AX7
The classic round Raven constructed with 24 vertical gores. It features a circular Velcro rip panel and Raven's patented side vent. There are probably more of these balloons than any other single type in the world.

Semco – various sizes, commonly AX7.
Mark Semich, builder of several Atlantic contenders, founded Semco, one of the pioneer US manufacturers. The Semco is a flat balloon composed of narrow vertical gores. The basket usually has a wooden base with an aluminium superstructure and canvas wall sides.

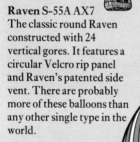

Barnes Firefly/ Dragonfly AX5 – AX7
The zig-zag diagonal patterns of the Barnes Firefly and Dragonfly tell the experienced observer of their factory of origin. They feature a parachute rip panel and a unique triangular basket, beautifully crafted in rattan cane.

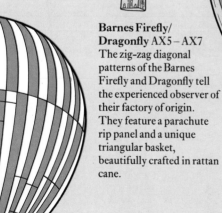

Thunder Z type
AX4 – AX7
A wide range of relatively 'flat' advertising balloons which are lighter than the competition (Cameron and Colt) models. The balloon has a parachute rip and the Thunder 40 series luxury basket is standard.

Adams AX7
Made by a small Georgia-based firm that produces neat balloon packages with the Adams multi-vent rip and vent panel. The basket design owes a lot to the Barnes philosophy of triangular construction.

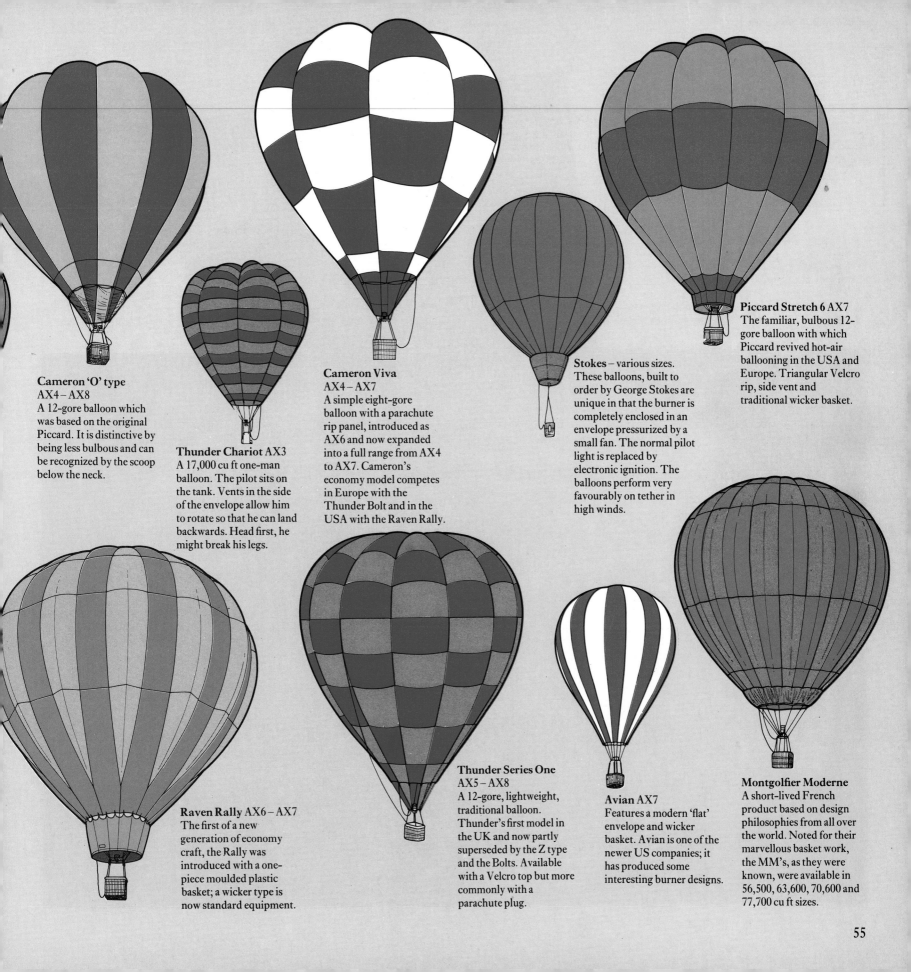

Cameron 'O' type
AX4 – AX8
A 12-gore balloon which
was based on the original
Piccard. It is distinctive by
being less bulbous and can
be recognized by the scoop
below the neck.

Thunder Chariot AX3
A 17,000 cu ft one-man
balloon. The pilot sits on
the tank. Vents in the side
of the envelope allow him
to rotate so that he can land
backwards. Head first, he
might break his legs.

Cameron Viva
AX4 – AX7
A simple eight-gore
balloon with a parachute
rip panel, introduced as
AX6 and now expanded
into a full range from AX4
to AX7. Cameron's
economy model competes
in Europe with the
Thunder Bolt and in the
USA with the Raven Rally.

Stokes – various sizes.
These balloons, built to
order by George Stokes are
unique in that the burner is
completely enclosed in an
envelope pressurized by a
small fan. The normal pilot
light is replaced by
electronic ignition. The
balloons perform very
favourably on tether in
high winds.

Piccard Stretch 6 AX7
The familiar, bulbous 12-
gore balloon with which
Piccard revived hot-air
ballooning in the USA and
Europe. Triangular Velcro
rip, side vent and
traditional wicker basket.

Raven Rally AX6 – AX7
The first of a new
generation of economy
craft, the Rally was
introduced with a one-
piece moulded plastic
basket; a wicker type is
now standard equipment.

Thunder Series One
AX5 – AX8
A 12-gore, lightweight,
traditional balloon.
Thunder's first model in
the UK and now partly
superseded by the Z type
and the Bolts. Available
with a Velcro top but more
commonly with a
parachute plug.

Avian AX7
Features a modern 'flat'
envelope and wicker
basket. Avian is one of the
newer US companies; it
has produced some
interesting burner designs.

Montgolfier Moderne
A short-lived French
product based on design
philosophies from all over
the world. Noted for their
marvellous basket work,
the MM's, as they were
known, were available in
56,500, 63,600, 70,600 and
77,700 cu ft sizes.

55

Inside a Cameron airship. Envelope construction is different to that of a spherical balloon; the gores are horizontal not vertical. The 96,000 cu ft airship is made of approximately 1,800 yds of fabric. Photographers are attracted by the potential of interior envelope shots.

Fashions in balloons; a variety of cuts and colours on private and commercial craft from all over the world.

The 65 ft-high crown of a balloon peeps over a hilltop as the author makes use of valley wind.

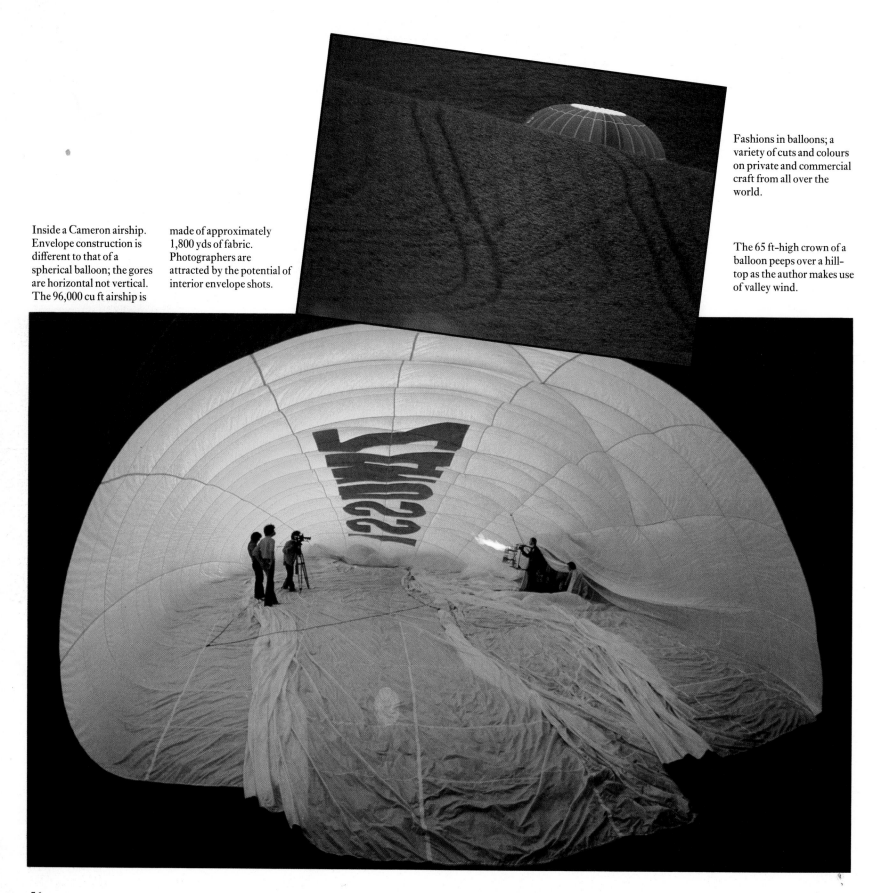

Construction/Envelopes

Containing a volume of light gas is most efficiently done in a sphere; the pressure against the outside atmosphere is evenly spread across all the envelope material. Thus most gas balloons are round, or close to it. But hot-air balloons are not sealed units and their shapes vary, influencing their flight characteristics.

There are three popular ways to construct an envelope: with horizontal, vertical or diagonal panels. All manufacturers use a network of load tapes or cords to carry the main load—the basket and its contents—with a fabric infill to contain the hot air. European makers favour light fabric and more load tape structure and Americans prefer heavier fabrics which share the load.

Envelope designs are controlled by the factors of cost, longevity and weight; but the principle of reducing fabric stress by producing a lightly curved gore is universal. Gores are sectional panels which are sewn into shape in the same way as spinnaker sails are constructed for racing yachts. As a curved face can take more pressure, the panels are cut so that the centre line of each gore is longer than its edges.

Only two kinds of yarn are suitable to make the fabric for hot-air balloons—nylon (polyamide) and Dacron (polyester). Dacron withstands higher temperatures, but nylon can be made stronger and lighter, thereby lessening the need for high operating temperatures.

The dispute as to which is more suitable is almost as old as man-made fibres. The argument is complicated by the fact that the finished envelope fabric is also dependent on the quality of weaving and coating.

Woven fabric is a mesh structure which allows air to pass through. To contain the air in a balloon, the fabric is coated with a material which seals the mesh. Polyurethane is commonly used, with additives such as silicone, a hard-wearing mineral, or neoprene, a synthetic rubber, to improve the 'handle' of the cloth. The coating is applied mechanically under pressure. The more coatings applied, the more air-tight the cloth becomes; but as coating makes the base material more fragile, there has to be a compromise between impermeability and strength.

Typical balloon fabrics weigh between 1·2 oz per sq yd and 2·4 oz per sq yd and have tensile strengths of 40–100 lb per inch-wide strip. Balloon manufacturers make their choices; and

relationships between shape, weight of fabric and gore pattern can produce an infinite variety of designs with the same margins of safety.

All coatings contain ultraviolet inhibitors to slow down degradation in sunlight. A common fallacy is that this also protects the yarn or base fabric. This is not the case; an ultraviolet inhibitor only protects the coating.

Vertical
As the design of vertical panel envelopes is constrained by the maximum width of fabric available, the number of gores needed to enclose a volume will vary. Only at the equator, or central line, is the panel width likely to exceed the fabric width. Some makers add gussets to this part of the gore but the system is inefficient in terms of design and labour time and is not in common use.

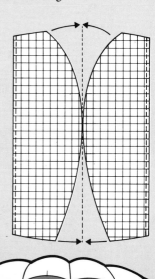

Horizontal
The panels are cut by hand from computer-generated templates. They vary in shape to take account of the pressure drop from the crown to the mouth of the balloon; the bottom panels are less curved and tighter.

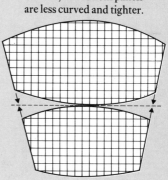

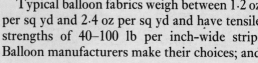

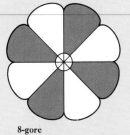

8-gore

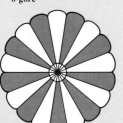

12-gore

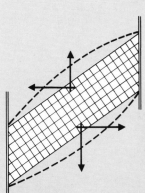

18-gore

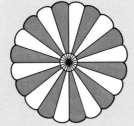

20-gore

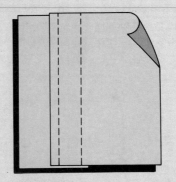

Double lap seam is used by all manufacturers to give strength and lightness. There are usually eight stitches to the inch.

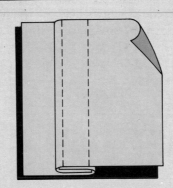

Flat seam with straight stitching is used only by Barnes. Typical of parachute construction, it is fast to sew and perfectly adequate.

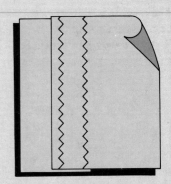

Zig zag is used by Thunder to achieve the strength of double lap with less fabric. Needle holes are farther apart, reducing the stress on the fabric.

Diagonal

Diagonal cut envelopes are more economical to make as they involve less wastage of fabric. Panels are cut out of the cloth diagonally but in straight lines with no curved edges. The curve of the inflated balloon is achieved by the fabric's tendency to stretch across the bias; a feature which is exploited by the clothing, parachute and sail industries to achieve shape. The only maker using this system is Barnes which produces a wide range in 12- and 18-gore styles with distinctive chevron patterns. The major disadvantage is that the application of graphics tends to distort the load pattern and make the balloon wrinkle. For commercial balloons, therefore, Barnes uses a flat-sided horizontal construction.

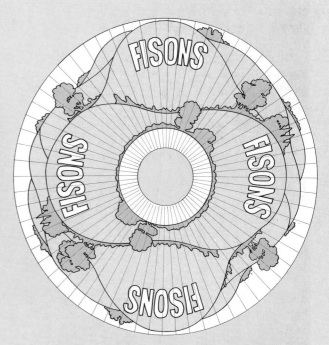

Appliqué is the process by which slogans and company logos are usually attached to an envelope, but large pieces of artwork, such as the field background on the Fisons balloon, are cut directly into the panels. Matching the design is complex and intermediate flat projection drawings are usually made. The scale is vast—the Fisons letters are five feet high. For smaller designs or short-term flag waving, acrylic spray paint is used. Some companies can instantly rename a balloon with ready-printed adhesive banners.

Jackson (right), 'son of *Jumpin' Jack'* is a Thunder 56 with parachute rip. Diagonal and vertical stripes are cut directly into the panels.

A Cameron 12-gore balloon (left) takes advantage of valley wind.

A Montgolfier Moderne being inflated. The taut crown line pulls the parachute open. The top half of this envelope is lined with aluminium fabric to prevent heat loss.

Confident that the air will be heated by the burner and contained by the envelope, the balloon pilot's main concern is with the control systems. The principle functions of the controls are to control descent by letting out hot air and to allow complete envelope deflation on landing. There are two main variants of the rip panel design available but the parachute, a comparatively recent development (c1971–72) has become the most important.

The basic idea of the parachute is simplicity itself. A circular hole is incorporated in the top of the balloon varying from 6-18 ft across, depending on manufacturer and balloon size. The hole is filled by a 'parachute' which is held centrally in place by restraining tapes inside the balloon. The hole remains closed, due to the internal pressure on the parachute and only opens when the operational line is pulled by the pilot to collapse the 'chute. Immediately the line is released, the parachute is sucked back into place, where the tapes ensure that it is seated correctly. This system has two main advantages. As it is a combined vent and rip panel it can be used as a vent for accurate and responsive in-flight control. It is also fail-safe. Almost every other type of rip panel requires, or should be equipped with, safeguards. The parachute is so fail-safe that it is now the dominant design for all new balloon types.

Whereas the parachute balloon has a single control system the older Velcro type employs two. The rip panel is an open or shut device sealed by Velcro (the fastening material which clings to itself on the burr principle) and is complemented by a vent for in-flight manoeuvring. The two operations of rip panel and vent panel are entirely separate. The Velcro rip panel is located in the crown of the balloon; the commonest version is the circular rip, although Piccard uses a triangular version.

Although Velcro is weakened by heat and water, the systems available are reasonably safe, provided the balloons are flown within well-defined limits. The swing away from this type of rip panel will probably become more pronounced as the advantages of the parachute become more widely appreciated.

The Velcro Company has taken steps to warn all balloonists that their product was not designed for balloons and can be unsafe, but balloon makers feel that their craft can be flown with a good margin of safety—providing they are well maintained. The big advantage of a Velcro rip panel is that it is fast in deflating the balloon and so it is particularly useful in the larger volume craft.

The Velcro rip panel is accompanied by a secondary opening area known as a vent or dump panel which is found in different locations on different makes of balloon.

On a hot day it is possible to hang in the air for several minutes in a normal balloon without using the burner. With a solar-heated balloon this time can be extended. Solar envelopes allow infrared energy to enter but not to pass out. The infrared enters through the transparent segment and heats a 'black body'—the opposite interior surface of the envelope. This absorbs energy and re-radiates it at a wavelength to which the transparent material is opaque. Another design uses a black envelope inside a transparent outer hull.

Since hot-air balloons operate at a low internal pressure and have to be much larger than gas balloons, there are advantages to making them longer and thinner. By enlarging the balloon's pressure head the envelope's resistance to turbulence is increased and its drag coefficient is lowered, thereby enabling it to climb using less energy.

In practice, the two extremes of conventional envelope design are represented by Raven's round balloons and Thunder's tear-drop shapes. The Raven uses marginally less fabric to enclose a given volume with a consequent reduction in surface area and heat loss. The Thunder climbs faster than a Raven and uses less energy in reaching a given altitude.

The net result is a similar fuel consumption but different in-flight handling characteristics, most of which are of marginal importance except to the expert. The Thunder reacts better in turbulence; the Raven can be flown in narrower wind bands with better opportunities for controlled steering.

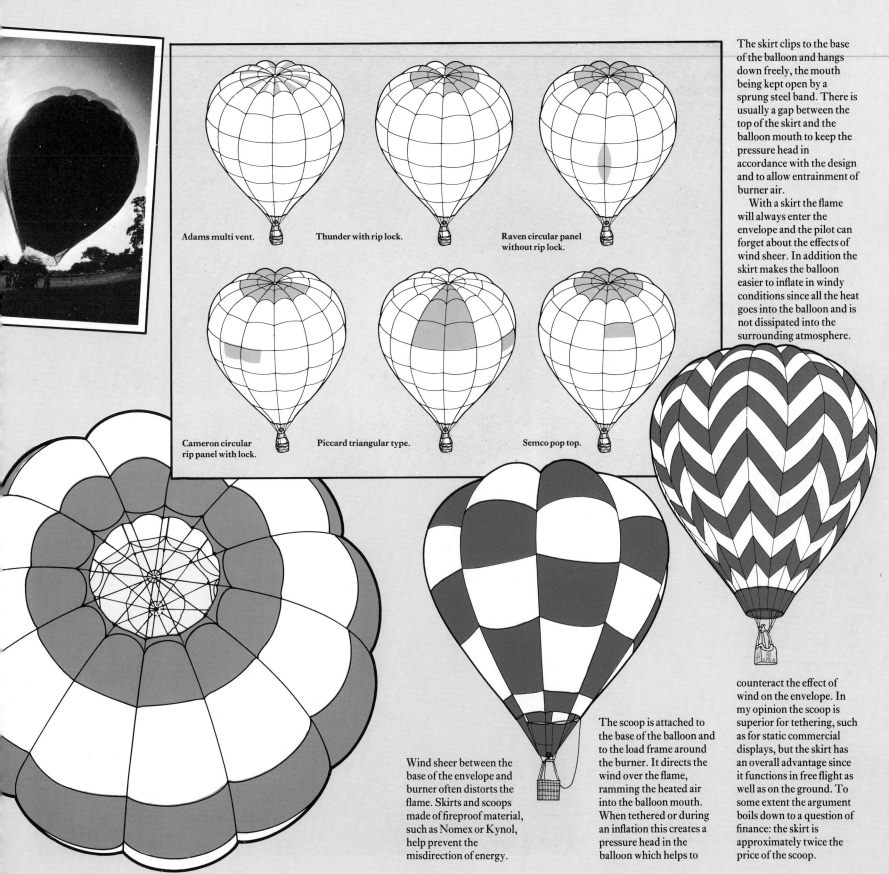

Adams multi vent.

Thunder with rip lock.

Raven circular panel without rip lock.

Cameron circular rip panel with lock.

Piccard triangular type.

Semco pop top.

The skirt clips to the base of the balloon and hangs down freely, the mouth being kept open by a sprung steel band. There is usually a gap between the top of the skirt and the balloon mouth to keep the pressure head in accordance with the design and to allow entrainment of burner air.

With a skirt the flame will always enter the envelope and the pilot can forget about the effects of wind sheer. In addition the skirt makes the balloon easier to inflate in windy conditions since all the heat goes into the balloon and is not dissipated into the surrounding atmosphere.

Wind sheer between the base of the envelope and burner often distorts the flame. Skirts and scoops made of fireproof material, such as Nomex or Kynol, help prevent the misdirection of energy.

The scoop is attached to the base of the balloon and to the load frame around the burner. It directs the wind over the flame, ramming the heated air into the balloon mouth. When tethered or during an inflation this creates a pressure head in the balloon which helps to counteract the effect of wind on the envelope. In my opinion the scoop is superior for tethering, such as for static commercial displays, but the skirt has an overall advantage since it functions in free flight as well as on the ground. To some extent the argument boils down to a question of finance: the skirt is approximately twice the price of the scoop.

Construction/Baskets

The wicker basket which provides a balloonist with his sky-high perch has remained virtually unchanged since the eighteenth century. Modern technology has been applied to burner, envelope and flight control systems but the comfort of a wicker basket has yet to be surpassed. In the early days of ballooning a variety of gondola styles were tried out, and in recent years some modern variations have appeared. But the creaking basket remains one of the most evocative of ballooning images.

An early Thunder basket made of rattan and willow was similar to baskets of 100 years ago.

Glaisher and Coxwell's gas balloon basket, equipped with trail rope and anchor.

The design was popular but the materials were not; this early Raven gondola in fibreglass and aluminium (far right) was later copied in wicker to give the crew more protection and comfort.

A typical balloon basket is made of rattan and willow, sometimes with a plywood floor. The edges are usually bound in rawhide, leather or suede, for protection against rough landings or handling. Stainless steel wires and/or upright rigid supports are used to attach the basket to the burner frame.

Continuing a ballooning tradition, Piccard, Cameron and other builders suspend the basket from a load ring which is in turn suspended from the envelope, and which doubles as the burner frame. The assembly is light but crude, with the disadvantage of being fully erect only when the inflated balloon takes the weight of the basket. As the balloon lands, the burner and frame may come down on the crew.

The early Raven model was not a basket at all but a lightweight gondola with a rigid frame constructed of aluminium and fibreglass. At the 1973 World Championships, European balloonists thought it looked frail and unsuited to its purpose. However, the design was popular with some American pilots—Denny Flodden actually won the championships in one. Despite its tendency to shatter on hard landings, the fact that it afforded little protection, and that tools and time were needed to take it to pieces, the Raven did have a clear advantage: the burner assembly did not collapse onto one's head when landing.

A major innovation came from Barnes, who introduced a range of triangular wicker baskets with some intriguing features. The burner is mounted on springs which allow lateral movement for convenience during inflation and flight. The principle of using ropes to carry the loads has been retained but thick cane uprights hold the burner in position.

The Barnes basket looks good and is both strong and functional. But there are two factors which do not suit European balloonists—the frame is not quickly detachable and the basket is comparatively large. In Britain, Thunder use a quickly demountable system incorporating load wires and rigid uprights and Cameron now offer a similar flexi-rigid design as an option.

Cameron flexi-rigid four-man basket

Barnes 40T rattan basket for three or four people

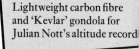

Lightweight carbon fibre and 'Kevlar' gondola for Julian Nott's altitude record

Raven Classic Ltd four-man basket

Traditional gas balloon basket

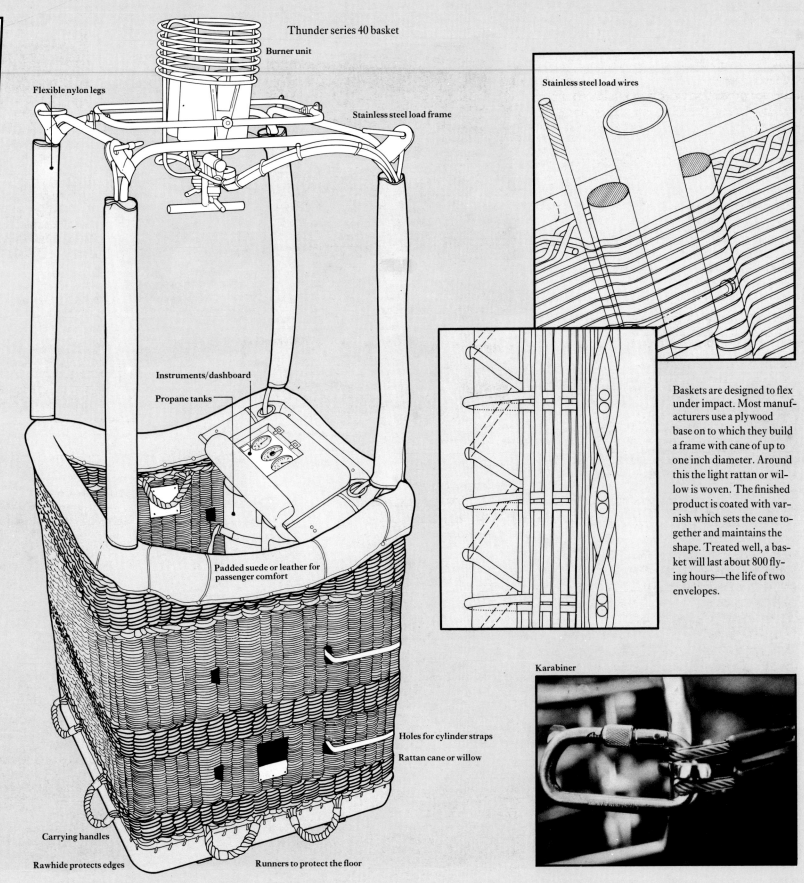

Thunder series 40 basket

Burner unit

Flexible nylon legs

Stainless steel load frame

Stainless steel load wires

Instruments/dashboard

Propane tanks

Padded suede or leather for passenger comfort

Holes for cylinder straps

Rattan cane or willow

Carrying handles

Rawhide protects edges

Runners to protect the floor

Karabiner

Baskets are designed to flex under impact. Most manufacturers use a plywood base on to which they build a frame with cane of up to one inch diameter. Around this the light rattan or willow is woven. The finished product is coated with varnish which sets the cane together and maintains the shape. Treated well, a basket will last about 800 flying hours—the life of two envelopes.

67

Hot air is not just warm; the temperature at the crown of an ascending balloon is about 100°C—the boiling point of water. To generate this heat, burners produce several million BTUs per hour. This is pure energy: none of it is absorbed by moving parts as is an engine's power. If the output of a 10 million BTU burner is converted to horsepower a staggering figure of over 4,000 bhp is achieved.

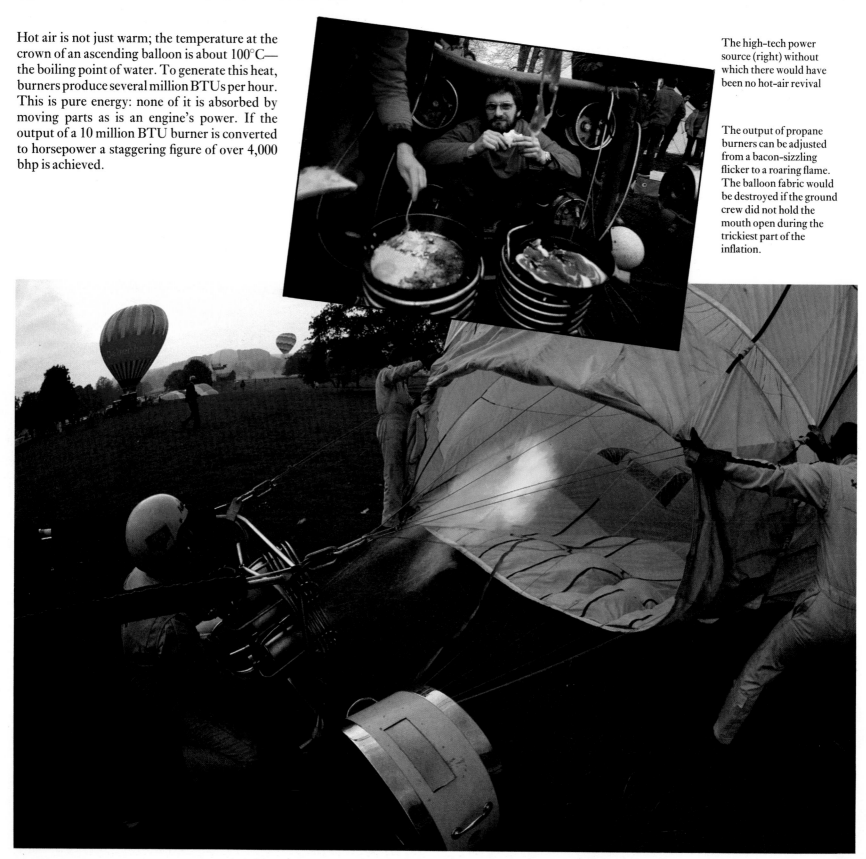

The high-tech power source (right) without which there would have been no hot-air revival

The output of propane burners can be adjusted from a bacon-sizzling flicker to a roaring flame. The balloon fabric would be destroyed if the ground crew did not hold the mouth open during the trickiest part of the inflation.

The powerhouse of every balloon is its propane burner—similar in principle to the butane burners used in cooking stoves. But if the gas was delivered as in a stove, the amount required to lift a balloon would freeze valves, hoses and cylinders before it had obtained enough heat from the atmosphere to vaporize.

A balloon burner, therefore, uses liquid propane which is vaporized in a stainless steel heating coil before it is ignited at the jets by a pilot flame. (The liquid itself would burn, but as a sooty and uncontrollable flame which is potentially harmful to the envelope.)

Burners are available with a range of power outputs to suit the various classes of balloon. Many of the accidents which happened in the early days were due to underpowered burners. Gradually, as in the evolution of internal combustion engines, power has been increased and weight significantly reduced. Most burners are single units which are usually coupled up to provide a twin power source, giving emergency power when needed and an independent back-up system should a unit fail.

The Barnes burner is more complex than most. It has three separate coil routes supplying three jets, but with only one main liquid supply. This unit cannot easily be coupled with another and the Barnes solution is to utilize a second supply jet known as 'Fire Two' which burns liquid only and can be used either for flying the balloon or as a booster.

All manufacturers use a constant-burning pilot flame (except the Stokes electronic ignition system), which operates either on vapour or from a direct liquid take-off.

One of the biggest differences between American and European designs is in the connections joining the fuel tank to the burner. Most Americans fit permanent hose couplings which require the use of tools when demounting. Typically, an American rig will be demounted once a year, whereas a European balloon system is disassembled after each flight.

Liquid valve: there are two types—regulated, which allows constant burning of an adjustable amount; and on/off (the more common type), used about six times a minute, for a total of 10–15 seconds, to keep the balloon in equilibrium.

Pressure gauge shows the gas pressure as it enters the burner coil. It indicates the amount of power available for a given length of burn. Typically this will read 40 psi on a cold day, 140 psi on a warm day.

The pilot light burns vapour off the top of the tank.

Jets through which vaporized liquid propane emerges. Usually designed to produce a flame with a fat base to heat the coil and a long, thin tip to enter the envelope.

Stainless steel vaporizing coil has to be capable of passing 5–10 lb of propane per minute to produce sufficient energy (6–12 million BTU/hr).

A typical layout with vertical 10-gallon tanks in a rectangular basket. The tanks may be interconnected, with two feeding one side of the burner and one tank the other.

A Raven layout using two 20-gallon tanks—one for each side of the burner—laid horizontally.

A triangular Barnes basket equipped with standard 10-gallon tanks.

There are only two types of cylinder in common use, although German regulations insist on a heavier version of the standard steel type.
The standard cylinder contains 40 lb of propane when full and weighs about 26 lb dry.
The Raven stainless steel type carries twice the amount of liquid. Its all-up weight of 120 lb makes handling difficult but it is virtually fireproof.

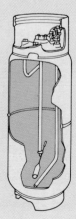

The variometer measures the rate of ascent and descent. It is available in mechanical or electrical form. The gauge is marked in feet per minute or metres per second and may be augmented by an audio signal to alert the pilot to dramatic changes in vertical speed.

Variometers work on the principle of pressure differential with altitude. They are used mainly to avoid excessive rates of climb and to monitor descent speed on landing. The normal scale reads 0–1,500 fpm (0–17mph).

The thermistor (or pyrometer) measures temperature at the crown of the balloon. It is an electronic thermometer with a probe connected to the gauge by a long wire. It serves the pilot by giving warning to him that the balloon's air is cooling; he knows that if the crown temperature drops the balloon will soon lose height.

The altimeter also works on the principle of pressure variation with height, but it measures the absolute height above sea level when adjusted to QNH, an international code figure provided by the local met. office or control tower. All aircraft flying in controlled airspace operate on QNH, enabling controllers to keep them separated.

Gauge has three needles marking in hundreds, thousands and tens of thousands of feet.

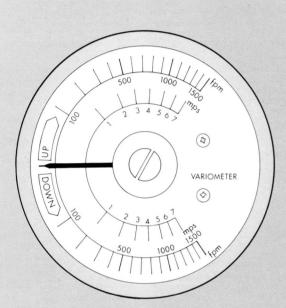

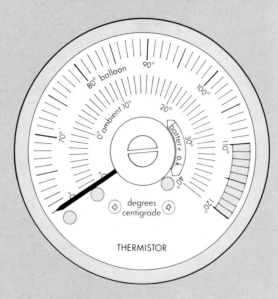

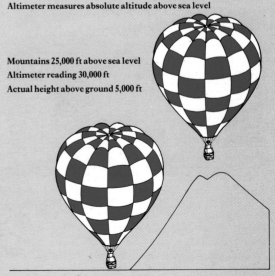

Variometer measures rate of change of altitude

Altimeter measures absolute altitude above sea level

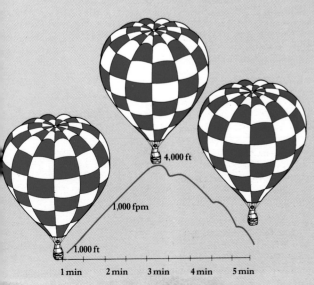

Probe at crown of balloon

Mountains 25,000 ft above sea level
Altimeter reading 30,000 ft
Actual height above ground 5,000 ft

Optimum temperature inside balloon is approx 100°C

Altimeter set for sea level

Selling pie in the sky

Is it a bird? Is it a plane? Is it a pie in the sky?—no, it's a special shape balloon hanging in the air.

Modern advertising frequently relies on surrealist techniques for shock effect, but for a long time commercial promoters have exploited the ability of familiar objects in unfamiliar settings to attract the attention of the public. When an image is seen hanging in the usually uncluttered sky, the incongruity creates interest.

Promotional, shaped balloons have been sent aloft since the earliest days of ballooning. The primary interest of balloon makers is to build efficient flying machines, but any shape, filled with hydrogen, will rise. In Paris during the late 1780s there was a craze for loosing inflated figures into the sky, among them flying horses and ladies in crinolines. But until recently promotional balloons have either been restrained by tether ropes or left to float away freely.

By the early twentieth century, Salmon's Tea had commissioned a lion rampant and an elephant to be flown over large public events in Britain.

Osram light bulb
The light bulb shape is well-suited for flying. Osram's version performs in a similar way to standard balloons and has been flown in a cross-Channel race.

Golly III
The first man-carrying special shape, with a volume of approximately 31,000 cu ft. The head is a conventional balloon below which is suspended the body—a large skirt of non-structural importance.

Champion spark plug
Amusing to watch lifting out into a wind from behind tree cover, this long thin shape enclosing 56,000 cu ft of air tends to bend in the middle. Again a large part of the body is a skirt.

Aerial advertising was revolutionized in the mid-1970s by the appearance of the first man-carrying 'shape'. This hot-air balloon, in the design of the famous Golly symbol of Robertson's jam, was fully capable of free flight and therefore able to attract considerable attention by appearing on schedule in front of audiences and pressmen.

The balloon world was divided in its reaction; those who favoured the new style of balloon as a logical extension of sponsorship were, in the main, professional operators trying to make a living. Some others thought the new development betrayed the essential simplicity of ballooning.

Public reaction, however, was good and several other sponsors followed, particularly in Britain, where a Champion spark plug and an Osram light bulb appeared. A pair of Levi jeans was commissioned for Holland, and in America a Kentucky Fried Chicken and a Greenpeace whale were made.

Although the jeans and spark plug were only vaguely related to traditional designs, most of the shapes have a strong resemblance to standard balloons, being based on straightforward three-dimensional geometric variations on a simple load-carrying structure with an extended skirt.

Special shapes receive certificates of airworthiness based on their ability to fly, and often the only restrictions imposed relate to the maximum windspeed in which they can be flown. The tolerant attitude of the British CAA is definitely one of the most important factors contributing to the rapid expansion of ballooning in the UK and there is a close, relaxed relationship between pilots, constructors and aviation authorities.

The Buzby balloon was built as part of a rather unnecessary campaign to advertise Britain's telephone service, but it makes good use of a series of simple shapes which are joined together to produce a close representation of the cartoon character.

The main body is recognizably that of a balloon, with a clearly defined network of vertical and horizontal load tapes on a flat-surfaced, multi-gore envelope. Instead of terminating at a crown ring, the top of the main balloon body is restrained by a horizontal tape at the junction between head and chest. The head

is a simple hemisphere, cut and sewn conventionally.

The arms, hands and telephone are all non-structural areas, inflated by bleed holes in the main envelope. These appendages could be removed, the bleed holes sewn up and the naked bird would still fly, probably better than it does with all the encumbrances.

Indeed pilots who fly Buzby report alarming flight characteristics. Fast, vertical ascents cause the balloon to pitch and toss, and on descents the arms and telephone tend to amplify the normal rotation. One pilot tells how he ascended from a showground faster than intended and found himself gazing at an artificial horizon of red and yellow fabric as the envelope pitched forward, dragging him horizontally behind.

74

Caraco ice cream cone
Built by Thunder for a Dutch customer this balloon has a 12-gore hemispherical top section with a long cone-shaped skirt. Due to its shape the balloon climbs like a rocket.

Levi jeans
Originally intended to be flown with a basket under each leg, it is more practical with a single gondola. The load wires attach approximately half way up the leg and there is a Velcro rip in the crown.

Gas flame
Great efforts were made by designers at Colt to ensure that the flame was asymmetrical in accurate imitation of the Segas symbol.

The commercial use of balloons is as old as ballooning itself. From the beginning of the sport men like Jean-Pierre Blanchard and Thaddeus Lowe were exploring the earning potential of ballooning, by obtaining sponsors and selling tickets to watch inflations. Advertisers quickly realized that a balloon makes an effective aerial billboard. Skywriting and banner flying were prohibited in Britain by the 1960s and so the new generation balloons were soon seen as a cost-effective way of exposing the maximum number of people to a trade-mark.

The first publicity hot-air balloons in the UK were built by Omega to advertise Nimble bread and their success is well proven by the continued use of the balloon theme. Years after the Nimble campaign had finished balloonists often found themselves greeted by the cry of 'Hey Mister— Is that the Nimble balloon you're flying?' This despite the fact that the balloon which they had just landed was completely anonymous. In America, balloon imagery is still used by Lark cigarettes—an association which stems from a highly successful advertising campaign of the 1960s.

As the 1970s progressed and ballooning became an increasingly well-publicized sport, so the number of opportunities to obtain sponsors increased. In 1974 the first Alpine crossing by hot-air balloon was paid for by Minolta cameras; not because the Minolta company had any particular interest in the flight but rather because the pilots convinced them that the balloon would be featured in *Time* magazine.

Sponsorship soon began to develop in two ways, to the benefit of both professionals and amateurs. Heineken breweries had pioneered balloon meetings as a form of publicity in 1972 and 1973 and, encouraged by the general reaction, they commissioned the *Gerard A. Heineken* which was, for a while, the largest hot-air balloon in the world. Among other achievements a new world record was set when a total of 33 passengers were carried. It still holds the World Duration Record for hot-air balloons, at over 18 hours. Its final curtain call came in 1979 when the worn-out balloon was sold off for one pound to the men who had flown it most— Cameron and Davey, the Atlantic pair. The Heineken brewery had run a well-planned programme. When they wanted to sell beer they flew the balloon.

Another way for a sponsor to fly his message is to back an amateur pilot. When Phillip Hutchins flies his balloons he happens to be advertising J & B Rare Scotch Whisky. Hutchins is a Buckinghamshire solicitor whose first balloon in the J & B colours appeared on national television in September 1974 when it was used for dropping hang-gliders to break new altitude records. This was followed by a well-publicized cross-channel race with another commercial balloon, *Motorway Tyres*. The balloon also earned newspaper column inches when it was flown in the Alpine race at the village of Chateau d'Oex. J & B now have three balloons: *Senior*, *Baby*, and *J & Big*—each of which is suitable for a particular type of flying. J & B balloon posters are to be found as far afield as Mexico City and these craft are well known in California. The operation has given the pilot and the sponsor great satisfaction and cost J & B very little.

By the mid-1970s many trade names were being floated past audiences at balloon meets, and the millions more who saw them on television. This development encouraged some pilots to commit themselves to professional ballooning. To give value to their sponsors, many take on newsworthy challenges. One British company specialized initially in record attempts, trying for World Duration, in the Fisons balloon, and the Women's World Altitude record in the Wrangler balloon. An attempt at crossing the North Sea ended with Julian Nott and his Typhoo balloon spreadeagled ingloriously across a tree on a windy Scottish coast. But the flight, and Typhoo tea, hit the headlines—as was intended. Another balloon, in the colours of British Bacon, slowly traversed Loch Ness trailing a side of bacon in the dark water as bait for the monster. The monster was not seen but the balloon appeared on television, radio and in newspapers. One great publicity success of the late 1970s was the Zanussi Atlantic crossing attempt. Zanussi made a name for itself out of ballooning failure.

In America the operation of balloons for publicity purposes grew more slowly, perhaps because most American pilots could afford to buy their own balloons without needing to find sponsors. Among several companies now operating balloons in America, one stands out: World Balloons of Albuquerque fly for many clients, including Budweiser and Anheuser Busch breweries. The Budweiser road show, complete with free beer dispensary, matching balloons, beer cans and trucks, is spectacular. Paul Woessner and Sid Cutter—1979 World and US National Champions respectively—have flying prowess which alone earns World Balloons and their sponsors tremendous publicity. After landing in first and second places in the World Championships in Sweden, Woessner and Cutter returned to a ticker-tape parade through Albuquerque city centre.

But it is the balloons rather than the heroes which attract the public and the sponsors. The trade-marks, logos and slogans which drift across the sky belong to a wide range of businesses, from multi-national, even nationalized, industries to provincial laundries. At the Swedish World Championships the British Champion was sponsored by the Schroder Life Insurance Company and the other two British crews by GEC and Debenhams Stores. They did not win and there were no ticker-tape homecomings. But the sponsors' names were seen in a 45-minute TV documentary.

In Germany, commercial ballooning is usually lower-key. One popular sponsor is a brewery which simply buys the balloon and gives it to the local balloon club with some running expenses.

Another ballooning activity which is growing in popularity is the 'airline' operation, taking fare-paying passengers for flights over scenic countryside. The best known is probably the Balloon Ranch in Colorado. Operating all year round, in snow and high heat, professional pilots and ballooning holidaymakers enjoy good flying and excellent facilities. In Europe the weather is rarely reliable enough for scheduled flying, though the enterprising resort of Chateau d'Oex in Switzerland runs an adventurous programme. Piloted by an ex-ski instructor, the Chateau d'Oex balloon lifts passengers into the exciting and rarefied world of high Alpine ballooning.

Perhaps the most successful passenger operations are the two East African safari services which carry up to 24 passengers a day across the Kenyan bush during nine months of the year. But those flights are rugged. The Bombard Society of Los Angeles organizes more civilized balloon outings over France, taking in vineyards, cellars, chateaux and the inevitable champagne.

CHARLIE BALLOON
Charlie
HONG KONG BALLOON AND AIRSHIP CLUB

SMIRNOFF CLOUDHOPPER
SMIRNOFF
VODKA
"Well they said anything could happen."

CLUB D'INTERVENTION AEROSTATIQUE
CIA
AUT PROGREDERE AUT MORE RE

CATHAY BALLOON
CATHAY PACIFIC
HONG KONG BALLOON AND AIRSHIP CLUB

MILTON KEYNES
BALLOON TEAM

GOLDFINGER BALLOON
Twilley's GOLDFINGER
G·BERD

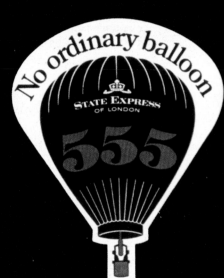

No ordinary balloon
STATE EXPRESS OF LONDON
555

LAMBERT & BUTLER
BALLOON TEAM
LB

COKE BALLOON
Coca-Cola
HONG KONG BALLOON AND AIRSHIP CLUB

"FLY AWAY WITH US... TO A WORLD WHERE ALL IS GOLD"
Terry's
ALL GOLD

SHELL BALLOON
HONG KONG BALLOON AND AIRSHIP CLUB

CLUB AEROSTATIQUE
DE L'ILE DE FRANCE

Backyard ballooning

The Montgolfier brothers' eighteenth-century experiments can be readily imitated in miniature. Model balloons, made of paper, effectively illustrate the simple principle of lighter-than-air flight. They can be purchased cheaply, but it is infinitely more fun to construct your own. The pleasure of making and chasing aerostats is heightened if there is competition. Build several and 'race' them.

The principle of hot-air balloons could not be more simple. Enclose a 'bubble' of warm air and it will float around until the warm air cools. Two people should be able to make a paper balloon in a couple of hours. All you need are 48 sheets of 12 in square tissue paper, glue, scissors and wire. To launch the results of your efforts, you will need an open space, preferably in the country, and a simple source of heat. Weather conditions will determine how far the balloon travels. One 'home-built' balloon survived four flights, flying as much as 50 miles on one trip.

The best way to inflate the balloon is with an electric fan heater, although a blowtorch, camping stove or even an open fire can be used.

To give the balloon a longer flight-span fix cotton balls, seeped in methylated spirits (denatured alcohol), to the crosswire. Light the fire just before take-off. There is obviously a fire risk with this method, and the balloon will fly perfectly well with just the original hot air.

When the balloon takes off, the game is to keep up with it. It can be a great sport on foot on a calm day, but in certain conditions, your 'bubble' could fly for miles and it is wise to have transport even if it is only a bicycle.

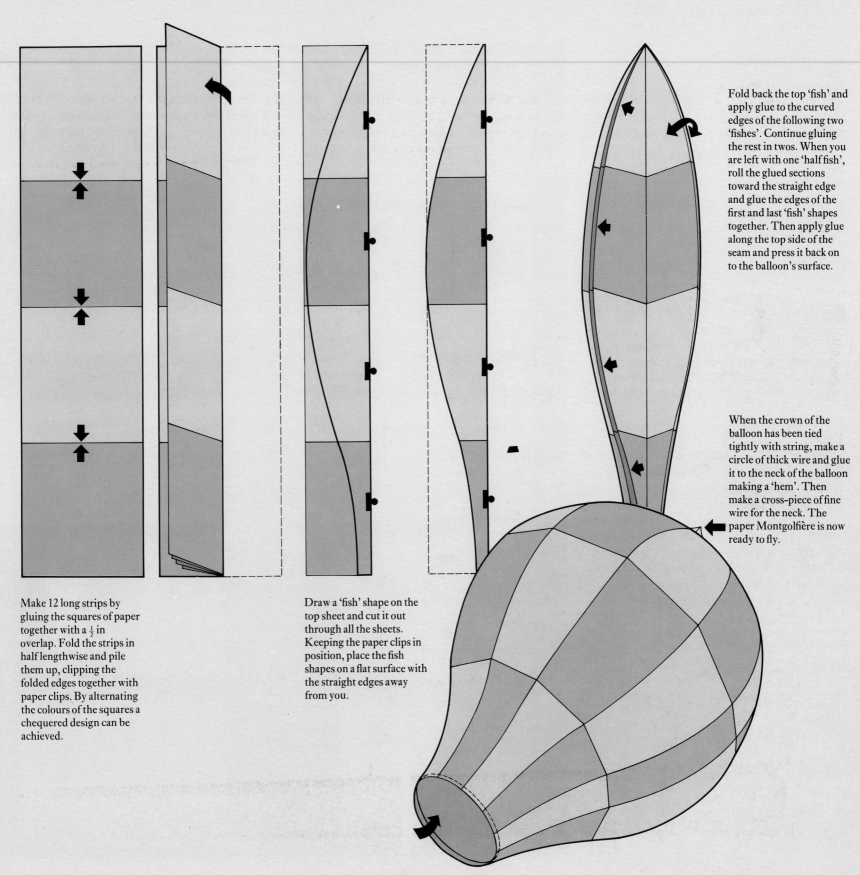

Make 12 long strips by gluing the squares of paper together with a $\frac{1}{2}$ in overlap. Fold the strips in half lengthwise and pile them up, clipping the folded edges together with paper clips. By alternating the colours of the squares a chequered design can be achieved.

Draw a 'fish' shape on the top sheet and cut it out through all the sheets. Keeping the paper clips in position, place the fish shapes on a flat surface with the straight edges away from you.

Fold back the top 'fish' and apply glue to the curved edges of the following two 'fishes'. Continue gluing the rest in twos. When you are left with one 'half fish', roll the glued sections toward the straight edge and glue the edges of the first and last 'fish' shapes together. Then apply glue along the top side of the seam and press it back on to the balloon's surface.

When the crown of the balloon has been tied tightly with string, make a circle of thick wire and glue it to the neck of the balloon making a 'hem'. Then make a cross-piece of fine wire for the neck. The paper Montgolfière is now ready to fly.

83

Aero-philately

The first airmail letter was carried in 1785 by Blanchard on his flight from England to France. The letter was written by William Franklin, royalist son of Benjamin and himself an ex-post office controller, who was living in exile in London; it was addressed to a younger member of the family, William Temple Franklin.

Many early balloonists carried letters as mementoes of flights and they frequently dropped messages overboard, but the random nature of lighter-than-air flight precluded the establishment of regular mail services. The one major exception was during the Siege of Paris in the Franco-Prussian war of 1870–71, when blockade-breaking balloons carried millions of letters out of the city.

The first scheduled mail flight took place on September 23, 1870, when a balloon loaded with letters made a three-hour flight from the French capital to Evreux. On landing, the pilot released carrier pigeons to return to Paris with news of his safe arrival. The pigeons carried letters and newspaper pages which had been photographically reduced on to miniature glass plates—the first use of microfilm.

Later on during the war the French interior minister planned to break the siege with a force of provincial soldiers. The plan to co-ordinate two attacks on the besieging army, one from within the city wall and another by 250,000 outsiders, was not a success; presumably because the letters carrying instructions were not delivered on time.

During the 1930s, airmail was carried on scheduled airship services but the most frequent use of balloon post has been the first day covers which are issued to commemorate historic or adventurous balloon flights. These are rarely handled by a regular mail service, but are more likely to be franked in the country of origin and carried in the balloon to be sold or given away at the end of a successful flight.

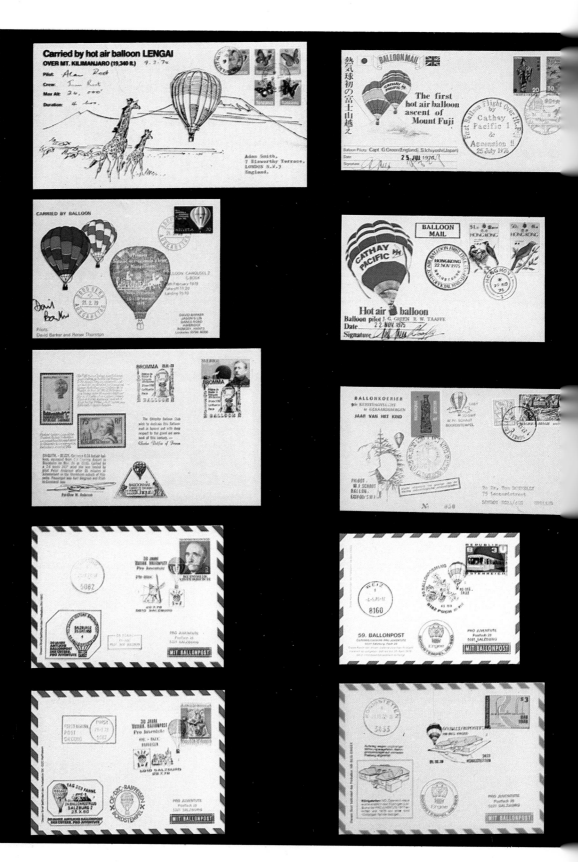

Sportsmen in the clouds

Once they had mastered the finer points of flying, eighteenth- and nineteenth-century balloonists went to extreme lengths to be the first to fly in a particular country, or to be the fastest, highest or farthest flier. Showmen and scientists broke most of the records and sportsmen had to indulge their taste for action in exploration rather than direct competition with other fliers.

Balloon rallies were commonplace in many countries, yet they were more often social, rather than competitive events. There was great public interest in ballooning, with spectators arriving in their thousands to watch inflations or stunts, but there were few attempts to organize ballooning as a spectator sport.

The only way achievement could be measured was by the distance or the duration of a flight. But to observe, organize, retrieve and publicize an event of any scale would have demanded a large investment and facilities for long-distance communication. In 1906 an American newspaper publisher with a nose for sensational sporting stories was to make his indelible mark on the world of ballooning by providing these necessary facilities for the first-ever international balloon race.

James Gordon Bennett, a millionaire in the grand style, was himself a sportsman who competed in sailing and equestrian events and provided trophies for motorboat and car racing. He also introduced polo to the USA and sponsored tennis tournaments. Bennett was a man of action who did not restrain himself from organizing the news he published. It was his paper which sent Stanley out to Africa to find Dr Livingstone; he also introduced weather reports to the daily press.

Having abandoned his patronage of the motor race series, Bennett turned his attention, and wallet, over to the sport of ballooning, inaugurating a series of international long distance races; the winner being the pilot who travelled farthest, measured in a straight line from the start.

The first race for the Gordon Bennett Aeronautic Cup was run on September 30, 1906, from Paris, with contestants setting off at intervals. An account of the race in the *Scientific American*, published the following month, listed the achievements of the sixteen entrants from seven countries who took off from Paris on that historic day. Santos-Dumont, the dirigible

pioneer, was one of the American team. He had entered a spherical balloon with some novel features, including a six-horsepower engine driving horizontal propellers to maintain altitude. However, he caught his arm in the gearing and had to descend after a short flight. Santos-Dumont, himself a millionaire, was a prize donor as well as competitor, but his award for the first flight over 48 hours duration was not claimed.

Another member of the American team, cavalry officer Frank P. Lahm won the race, flying across much of England to land near Whitby, in Yorkshire, a distance of 395 miles, in 22 hours 28 minutes. Lahm only descended when he did because he had reached the North Sea coast.

Most of the balloons had been specially made for the race, indicating the interest among aeronauts. The public's fascination had also been evident; 250,000 had reportedly watched the ascents, and millions read about the race in the press—including the readers of the New York *Herald*, Gordon Bennett's paper.

Following the original intention, the next race was started in America, the home country of the winner; it was won by a German and in 1908 the event was flown from Berlin. The winner on that occasion was a Swiss pilot whose flight of 43 hours deposited him in the sea off the coast of Norway. As the race was one of endurance and the craft at the mercy of the wind, many pilots experienced the strange hospitality of foreign lands. In 1912, while a Frenchman established a record of 1,495 miles, an American pilot was imprisoned when he landed in Russia. In 1934 five balloons went missing in that country but they were safely accounted for after a week.

The dramatic events which occurred did not

detract from the public's interest—far from it. The races were held 26 times up to the outbreak of World War II and to the world Gordon Bennett was now synonymous with balloon, rather than car, races. The 1938 race was the last major event of the gas balloon era. Another event was scheduled for the following year but, as stipulated in the rules, it was to take place in the country of the previous winner. Antoni Yanusz, victor in 1938, was Polish; the race was scheduled for September 1939. On the first day of the month Hitler invaded Poland....

In 1979, after 41 years, the spirit, challenge and name of the Gordon Bennett races were invoked once again as a race for gas balloons was held at Long Beach, California. Not surprisingly the event attracted some of the most experienced gas balloonists in the world. Seventeen of the 18 entrants, however, were completely outflown by the balloon *Double Eagle III*, piloted by Abruzzo and Anderson, the men who flew the Atlantic. Their 583-mile flight must have seemed like a picnic outing in comparison with the ocean trip. They landed in Colorado, just 52 minutes short of the 48-hour challenge which Santos-Dumont had made for the first race in 1906.

The old hydrogen balloons took up to 12 hours to fill. At big rallies or meetings they were laid out in rows to be fed by one umbilical pipe. Observers were kept well away from the inflammable gas. The small hydrogen balloons can be inflated without the need for shelter on a windy day.

How can you race balloons? They are virtually unsteerable, and they travel at the pace of the wind. But, the competitive urge being as strong as it is, balloonists have devised a range of close-quarter contests as tests of flying skill rather than stamina.

To understand how balloonists compete against each other one must discard the notion of the winner always being the first past the post. Since balloons are at the mercy of the atmosphere, all travelling in the same airstream at more or less the same speed, balloon racers have to be accurate rather than fast. The winner is the balloonist who comes closest to a target—either by landing on it or by dropping a marker to fix his notional landing point.

As with ocean racing or cross-country skiing it is difficult for the spectator on the ground to judge the progress of a race since the racing does not necessarily involve position relative to other balloons but position overall.

In the northern hemisphere the wind generally veers to the right with height. And the words 'Right with height' are drummed into every learner pilot's head. Race theory, then, is simple. A target is chosen downwind of the launch site and the balloon pilot gains altitude to turn right and flies low to regain left, zig-zagging through the sky while aiming for the target.

In practice, the atmosphere is eccentric in its behaviour. It is a pilot's skill in sensing the vagaries of the wind on a given day that wins the prizes.

While ground crews can revel in the magic of a new day, the pilots are intent on plotting courses—one eye on the map, the other on the wind indicators.

Hare and Hounds. In this race the hounds try to land or drop a marker as close as possible to the landing position of the hare. The competitors are briefed on the estimated flight time for the hare balloon which is launched on its own. Competitors take off from the same field some 10–15 minutes later.

Judge Declared Goal. The pilot flies to a goal downwind and drops his marker. The winner is the closest to the goal. In the early days of racing only one goal was set but the one-target race has been superseded by the multiple target version (or Hesitation Waltz). The pilot chooses his most appropriate goal when actually in the air. The result of this variant has been to produce some amazingly accurate flying. Pilots as good as World Champion Paul Woessner have achieved zero ft—putting the marker in the centre of the target cross.

FIFO (Fly In Fly On). Often combined with the Judge Declared Goal to extend the race. The pilot chooses a second goal in flight and notes its grid reference on the marker he drops on the first target. He then flies on to this predetermined point and drops a second marker to score.

Pilot Declared Goal. Similar to Judge Declared Goal except that the pilot chooses his own target. (By tracking helium-filled party balloons with a compass a course can be plotted to produce a likely goal.) Thereafter the pilot is on his own: though the wind may alter, the declared goal cannot be changed and a pilot cannot use his sky neighbours as wind guides since he will not know what targets they have chosen. A most difficult form of racing!

CNTE (Controlled Navigational Trajectory Event). Known in Europe as the Fly In, this is the most fascinating race for spectators. The launch field becomes the goal and the competitors are dispatched to take-off from beyond a certain distance. In this race, as in the Pilot Declared Goal, an individual's advantage is determined by his skill in planning a flight path. Spectators standing at the goal can observe the effects of wind variation with height as balloons make their approach from all angles.

Barograph Race. In the first and second World Championships barograph races were run but they were difficult to organize and sometimes dangerous. A major problem was the cost of providing enough barographs—instruments which record time against altitude. Each pilot is given a barograph with a smoked aluminium plate inside, on which a course is outlined. He has to keep the needle of the barograph pen tracing a course inside the limits shown on his plate and is scored on the number of seconds he remains within the limits.

Big Bender or Elbow. This race involves changing course as acutely as possible. Balloons fly out for a specified minimum distance, for example 5 miles; the pilot drops a marker to indicate his position and then flies the second leg, attempting to change course as much as possible. This is one of the least spectacular races for onlookers because the balloons scatter over wide areas of countryside. But for the pilots it is an exciting race: on a typical day they may climb to between 10–15,000 ft in an effort to find 'Right with height'.

Race to a Line. The one exception to the rule— a race where speed is essential. Balloons are timed to a finishing line. The winner is the fastest. It is possible to gain speed by climbing, but the wind currents higher up may not be in the right direction. The problem facing the pilot is to discover where his fastest course lies, particularly when the finish line is angled to the wind. Differential times are sometimes seconds but often minutes, even on a short flight.

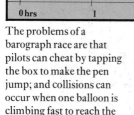

The problems of a barograph race are that pilots can cheat by tapping the box to make the pen jump; and collisions can occur when one balloon is climbing fast to reach the next box while a near neighbour is descending.

On one occasion my co-pilot was monitoring our vertical descent speed which was about to take us out of the lower box, when a balloon soared past us, burner full on. The crew, fully aware of our presence, were helpless. They had passed within 50 ft of our envelope at a collision speed approaching 3,500 ft per minute.

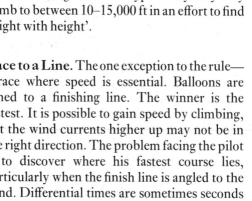

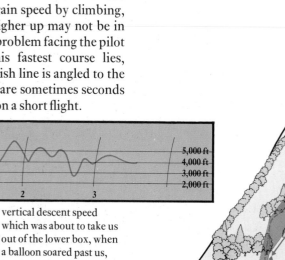

Hare &

Hare balloon is visible to hound

Hound is sucked into hillside

Valley wind sto
Hare climbs to
Hound follows

Hare finds valley wind

Start

Barograp

5,000 ft
4,000 ft
3,000 ft
2,000 ft

0 hrs   1   2   3

Valley

Ground

Upper

Start

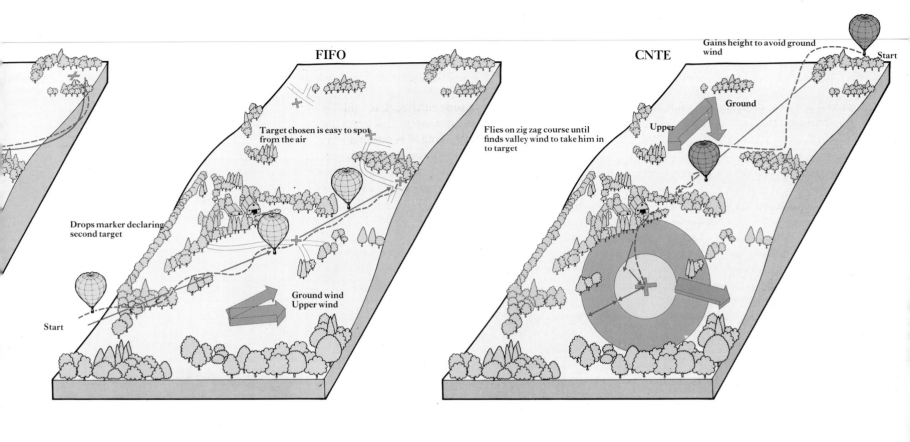

FIFO

Target chosen is easy to spot from the air

Drops marker declaring second target

Ground wind
Upper wind

Start

CNTE

Gains height to avoid ground wind

Start

Ground

Upper

Flies on zig zag course until finds valley wind to take him in to target

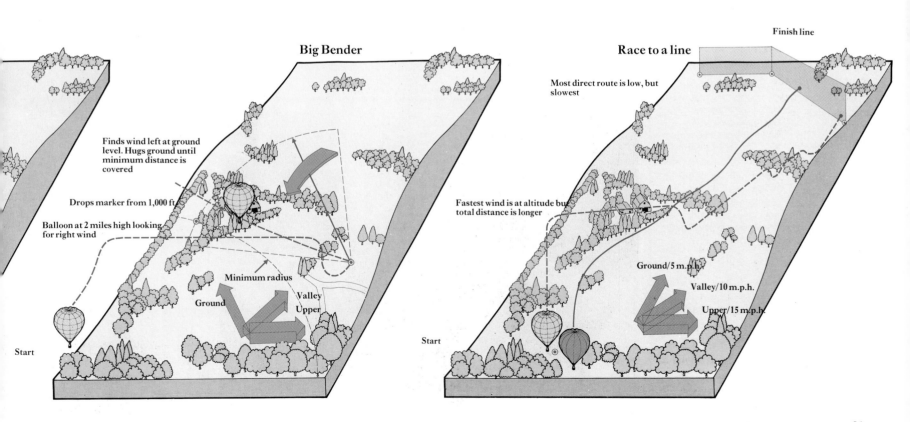

Big Bender

Finds wind left at ground level. Hugs ground until minimum distance is covered

Drops marker from 1,000 ft

Balloon at 2 miles high looking for right wind

Minimum radius

Ground

Valley
Upper

Start

Race to a line

Finish line

Most direct route is low, but slowest

Fastest wind is at altitude but total distance is longer

Ground/5 m.p.h.

Valley/10 m.p.h.

Upper/15 m.p.h.

Start

Ballooning—especially competitive balloon flying—is about understanding and exploiting the weather. The methods used are many and various.

Met. Balloons

To determine the wind's direction an experienced pilot will often release helium-filled party balloons and by recording time against altitude he can 'guesstimate' what he will find aloft. He will know that the balloon climbs at, say, 500 fpm and can therefore plot directions at varying altitudes.

Target Smoke and Target Approach

Good balloon pilots are capable of steering their craft with a reasonable degree of accuracy through a narrow band of wind about the main flow and most competitive pilots can land within 200 yds of a goal. Most problems occur in the final approach to the target because the wind is fickle; either smooth flowing or turbulent, it runs like a river over trees, houses and hills. Many competent flights are ruined by a moment's carelessness at the last minute and unlike other forms of sport the pilots cannot make an about turn and try again. In ballooning you have only one chance.

The wind is capricious below 250 ft, and many pilots plan their approach to arrive at 250 ft over target and to 'drop like a brick', releasing the marker as close as possible to the target. Last-minute wind indicators, such as chimney smoke, help and an efficient ground crew may set off a smoke bomb to show the effects of local turbulence.

During flight the pilot or navigator plots an approach track to the target based on estimated speeds at various altitudes. For the last 500 yds flying is mostly intuitive and careful plans are discarded as local turbulence becomes visible.

The **Task Setter** is essentially the boss. He plans the tasks, issues briefings to pilots, supervises the launch officials and the scoring. If a pilot disagrees with his score his first recourse is to the task setter.

The **Chief Observer** and **Observer Corps** are there to ensure that pilots do not cheat. These people either fly with the pilots or observe from the ground. Their role is that of impartial policemen and public relations officers. They also measure the pilots' scoring position, to compute race positions.

The **Met. Officer** obtains meteorological forecasts from surrounding stations, compiles information and advises the task setter on which type of race would be most suitable.

The **Safety Officer, Launch Director** and **Launch Officials** are the people seen at balloon races in fluorescent jackets. They are responsible for launch safety and crowd control.

The **Chief Scorer** and **Scorers** process the observer information to produce the results. Distances are commonly measured by tape or, as in recent World Championships, by laser. In most countries results are now processed by computer to plot the exact distance in metres and millimetres from marker to target.

Laser measuring equipment is centred on the yellow cross (below). Observer in foreground uses a tape measure. Orange markers on the grass have been dropped from balloons.

Seen from a competing hound balloon in a hare and hounds race, the hare crew lay out the yellow target cross (right) before their balloon is deflated. The other two balloons will be blown past off course.

French champion Michel Bergounioux collects a souvenir signature from an American team member (right). Nigel Tasker (task setter) launches a met. balloon at a briefing. The red flag warns that hot inflations are not allowed because the wind is too strong.

During the 1970s balloon racing developed into a well-organized sport with international rules by which the pilots' ability could be measured. American aeronauts had established a set of basic rules which were applied in 1963 to the first US National Championship. Ten years later the world's first international event took place in Albuquerque, New Mexico.

Organized by the Cutter family, in particular Bill and Sid, with the help of Ed Yost and others, the event was billed as the World's First Hot-Air Balloon Championship. The winner was Denny Flodden, an American. Second place was taken by Bill Cutter himself, third by Janne Balkedal of Sweden and the highest-placed Englishman was Terry Adams in fifth place. Half of the total points were awarded for a barograph race, a type of competition with which only the Americans were familiar, so many Europeans returned home feeling that the event was biased in favour of the American entrants, while the Americans began planning the next event to prove that they could win again just as easily.

In Britain the first Nationals were organized in May 1975 as a method of selecting the British team for the next World Championship to be held in September of that year, but again the Americans won—this time Dave Schaffer, flying his home-built balloon, touched down as undisputed winner. Second place went to Janne Balkedal, third to Vizzard of Australia and the four-man British team gained fourth, fifth and sixth places. The standard of competition had improved since the previous championship but there were many organizational changes still to come.

The next major landmark in competitive ballooning was the British National Championship in 1976 where a new set of rules devised by two English pilots, Nigel Tasker and Martin Moroney, was used for the first time. Included in the new rules was a provision for independent observers to record pilots' movements and the introduction of markers for pilots to drop on to targets, instead of actually landing.

With little modification these prototype rules were retained for the 1977 World Championship which, at the request of the BBAC, was held in Britain at Castle Howard, Yorkshire. The ballooning world remembers those September days for some of the best flying ever and the pilots remember the championship as a real test of skill.

Despite the British team's practice, it was another American walk-over. First place went to Paul Woessner from Albuquerque and second to Bruce Comstock of Michigan. Although the Americans had fielded a strong team of 10 balloons, this championship had proven to be a straight contest between Woessner and Comstock, who was already US National Champion.

The fourth World Championship was staged by the Swedes at Uppsala in 1979 during the coldest European winter for many years. Once again, the contest was between Woessner and the Rest with Sid Cutter (son of Bill) in second place, Roux-Devillas of France in third and Alan Dorman representing Britain in fourth place.

Between 1973 and 1979 there were four World Championships. The Americans won each time, with Woessner taking two out of the four titles. Over the same period there were seven National Championships in the USA, four of which were won by Comstock. In Britain there were four National Championships, two of which were won by Crispin Williams with Tom Donnelly a close second in three of the events. A recognizable breed of competition balloonists was beginning to evolve.

Denny Flodden, 1973 World Champion, in an 'unsuitable' lightweight basket.

Dave Schaffer, 1975 World Champion, in a home-built balloon.

Paul Woessner (centre of picture) receives his prize at the 1977 World Championships.

The variation of wind direction with altitude can be enormous. In one of the best-known racing areas in the world, Albuquerque, New Mexico, where two World Championships have been staged, balloonists have discovered the phenomenon known as 'The Albuquerque Box'—a pattern of winds in which a balloon can be turned at right angles with a height change of as little as 50 ft. Even novices can manoeuvre their craft around this desert and mountain country with ease, sometimes landing after a flight of two hours just a few feet from the original take-off site.

The unique weather conditions have led to the creation of a series of races which are peculiar to Albuquerque. One of the most intriguing variants of the target race is Albuquerque Blackjack. Squares marked on the ground are given the values of playing cards and competing pilots have a certain number of drops to score twenty-one or, as can

always happen, go bust. This kind of accuracy in flying needs the peculiar box conditions which exist nowhere else in the world. It is perhaps no coincidence that this city has provided a World Champion and a US National Champion as well as the first men to cross the Atlantic by balloon.

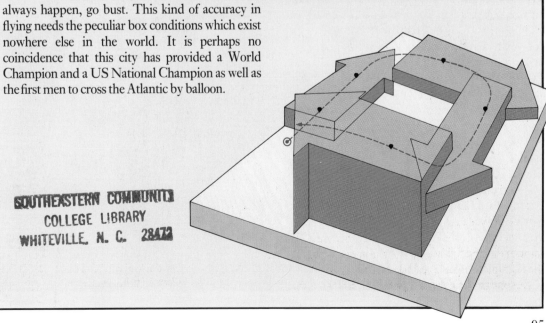

Per Lindstrand, balloon builder   Chris Davey, Atlantic pilot   Michel Bergounioux, French champi

Alan Dorman, UK Champion '77   Simon Faithfull, Dutch Champion   Alan Noble, *Aerostat* editor   Don Cameron, balloon builder   Freddy Eshoo, pil

Nigel Tasker, Championship director   Anneke Sandel, women's altitude record holder   Kevin Meehan, examiner   Terry Adams, balloon builder

Robbie Noirclerc, balloon builder   Dick Wirth, UK Champion '76, and Tom Donnelly, balloon builders   Julian Nott, altitude record holder

Solo stats

One morning in 1977 the American aeronaut Brian Boland appeared at Thunder Balloons carrying a suitcase and a backpack. Inside the case was a vacuum-packed balloon envelope; in the pack was a miniature burner.

Brian had flown from the States with the complete balloon as hand baggage. Within a week he had woven himself a one-man basket and he flew the complete rig at the Castle Howard World Championship meet. Boland balloons are some of the smallest in the world and they are flown with great success by Brian and his wife Kathy, who hold altitude and duration records in AX1, AX2 and AX3 classes.

Individual balloons, or 'solo stats', provide pilots with an amazing degree of freedom. It is possible to make a complete flight, from take-off to retrieve, without the assistance of even one crew member. Boland's *Piccolo* has a ready-to-fly weight of only 90lb.

Considering the advantages of portability and low cost, it is surprising that these small aerostats are not more popular, but until recently none have been on sale to the public.

The first Raven balloon which inspired the hot-air revival, the Vulcoon, was a single-seater of 31,000 cu ft. A tubular steel frame chair straddled a pair of gas tanks and the air was heated by a glorified blowtorch.

Bobby Sparks continued the small balloon tradition with *Baby Lark*, beneath which he was suspended on a harness with a small gas tank on his back. The first balloon built by Maurice Chaize was similar to the Vulcoon with the added sophistication of a control by which the pilot's chair could be turned.

More recently Colt produced the Cloud-hopper for Smirnoff Vodka; 12,000 cu ft of polyester-enclosed hot air lifts a lightweight frame which can be rotated. As a safety precaution the pilot can release the parachute harness which holds him to the machine.

The Thunder Sky Chariot was influenced by earlier types but the balloon, the first individual model to be generally available, has several unique control features. Four vents allow clockwise and counter-clockwise rotation and fuel gauges are read via a mirror. The 17,000 cu ft Chariot is big enough for extended flight yet it can be packed onto a car roof rack. Initial interest has been encouraging, with most early sales being made to owners of conventional craft.

Boland's 12,000 cu ft balloon *Piccolo* (top left) is a small AX2, designated 'experimental' by the FAA. Maximum flight time is 30mins on 5 gallons of fuel. After flying from his Connecticut backyard, Boland hitchhikes home. Motorists are often intrigued by his equipment bundle and aeronaut's costume.

The XXUS-sponsored AX3 balloon (left) was used by Brian and his wife Kathy to establish world altitude records in 1978.

The Colt Cloudhopper, built for Smirnoff Vodka, skims the water during its introduction to the British press. The harness rig contrasts with the more common system of using the tank as a seat. The Sky Chariot (right) provides more comfort and protection for the solo aeronaut.

Far out flying

The

Thursday, Aug. 17, 1978

Americ

Menagerie Comes to

ANIMALS, ANIMALS — Five-year-old Sherri Bardascini
of 18 Pine St., Amsterdam, has a chance to pet a goose at
Mother Nature's Menagerie, which is on the east side of

Amsterdam Board
For Expansion of

By PHILIP BROWN
Recorder News Staff
AMSTERDAM — The
Greater Amsterdam Board of
Education last night
authorized paying the Stetson
Partnership of Utica up to
$2,000 to develop detailed
plans for expanding Bacon
Elementary School.
Board members said the
expansion might enable the

district is maintain the
"neighborhood" concept of
elementary schools as well as
save money by reducing
busing.
Previously the board had
considered expanding Bartley
and McNulty elementary
schools to accommodate
students from Academy Street
and Florida schools. Under
that plan some 300 students

Settlement Reported N
In Bitter Memphis Strik

MEMPHIS, Tenn. (UPI) —
Mayor Wyeth Chandler and
the vice president of the
firefighters' union said today
a settlement was near in
Memphis' bitter police and
firemen strike.
The mayor said early today
that negotiators were "very
close" to reaching an

agreement to end the dual
strikes and he repeated the
statement later in the morning
during an interview.
Representatives of the two
unions held marathon
meetings into the small hours
of the morning, with federal
mediator Ed McMahon sitting
in on some of the talks.

President Move

WASHINGTON (UPI) — A
deeply concerned President
Carter plans to move rapidly
in an effort to bolster the
beleaguered dollar, whose
value continues to plunge on
the foreign exchange markets.
The chief executive has
called on Treasury Secretary
Michael Blumenthal,
Chairman William Miller of
the Federal Reserve Board
and other economic advisers
to recommend solutions to the
dramatic decline

The White House declined to
say whether Carter set a
deadline, but in view of the
monetary crisis, he was expected to take action soon.
Carter called an emergency
meeting Tuesday after the
dollar hit new lows in Japan,
Germany, Switzerland and
Holland, to express "deep
concern over developments in
foreign exchange markets in
recent days."
"The sharp decline in the
dollar and disorderly market

Balloonists are continually seeking new ways to enjoy the oldest form of aviation. Sometimes, as with flights over Africa, they have been pre-empted in theory—Jules Verne's *Five Weeks in a Balloon* was about a transafrican flight 100 years ago. His characters intended to make use of trade winds and, in advance of the many Atlantic crossing attempts, the balloon was to be a combination hot-air/hydrogen type.

The real adventure for most balloonists is simply flying in foreign airspace, across borders and cultural boundaries, with only a guess at the destination. The essential differences of lifestyle are fascinating. Yet these differences, when manifested in bureaucratic procedure, are often the balloonist's biggest headache.

The first flight in Nepal, organized by Dutch broadcaster Hans Zoet, had been virtually abandoned until Zoet met the king's helicopter pilot who cut through red tape and made that flight possible. Without similar strokes of fortune, many other 'far out' flights would not have left the ground.

The great Atlantic challenge

'. . . our friends at Paris will come flying through the air instead of ploughing the ocean.'

George Washington 1784.

One free-flight crossing is, so far, ballooning's only successful response to George Washington's vision of an aerial connection between America and Europe. The Atlantic Ocean remains, even now, nearly 200 years later, the Great Challenge of Ballooning. Thaddeus Lowe made preparations for a crossing in the days before the American Civil War but there is little of true significance until the 1950s when four Britons, Colin Mudie, his wife Rosemary, Bushy Eiloart and his son Tim planned a trip, using their experience as transatlantic sailors. They embarked on an east–west attempt from Tenerife, off north-west Africa, riding the southern trade winds. *Small World* took off on the night of December 12, 1958, and soon broke the existing balloon duration records. A frightful storm ditched the crew into the Atlantic and they completed their journey (another 1,450 miles) in the balloon's gondola to arrive in Barbados on January 5.

Not only had they tried to fly from east to west, they had planned this epic journey at a time when ballooning of any type was virtually non-existent outside a small European clique. The adventurers had designed, constructed and learnt to fly the balloon with minimal assistance. In England there was not even one qualified balloon examiner: Eiloart's licence was granted by a CAA examiner who followed the qualifying flight on a bicycle.

Mudie's major contribution to transoceanic ballooning was to design a gondola which would survive a high speed ditching in rough weather. When his team ran into a cumulo-nimbus cloud 94½ hours out, they cut the balloon away and splashed down in comparative comfort. The sound, advanced design of *Small World* was to be copied for future attempts over two decades—a prototype and an inspiration.

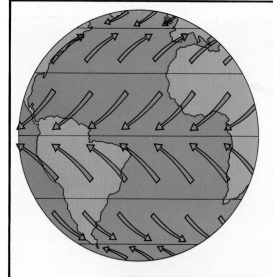

The trade winds blow from east to west in the southern Atlantic and in the opposite direction from America's northern shores. At a higher altitude, the 'rivers in the sky', discovered by John Wise in the 1860s, later attracted Gatch and Forbes who attempted to ride the 'jet streams'. But the trade winds, which had carried the old sailing clippers before them, finally blew the first balloon between the old and new worlds.

In contrast with the almost instinctive approach of the *Small World* team, the successful satellite-monitored flight of *Double Eagle II*, 20 years later, made use of westerly trades and avoided the type of Atlantic depression in which *Small World* foundered.

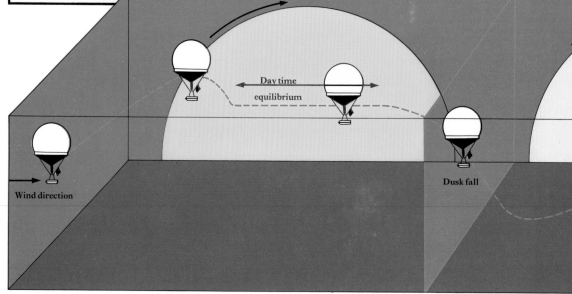

Day time equilibrium

Wind direction

Dusk fall

Day time
The heat of the sun expands the gas, reducing its density. The balloon rises. The craft stabilizes when internal pressure is equal to atmospheric pressure (this may be caused by the pilot venting gas). The balloon is now in day-time equilibrium.

Night time
As the gas cools it becomes more dense causing the balloon to descend.

The pilot drops ballast to counter the fall. The balloon rises slightly and settles into night-time equilibrium. On *Small World* sea water was to be winched aboard at daybreak and jettisoned as ballast at night.

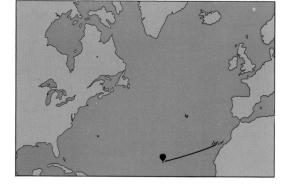

The flight of *Small World* ended after 1,200 nautical miles. For the rest of the journey she became a ship.

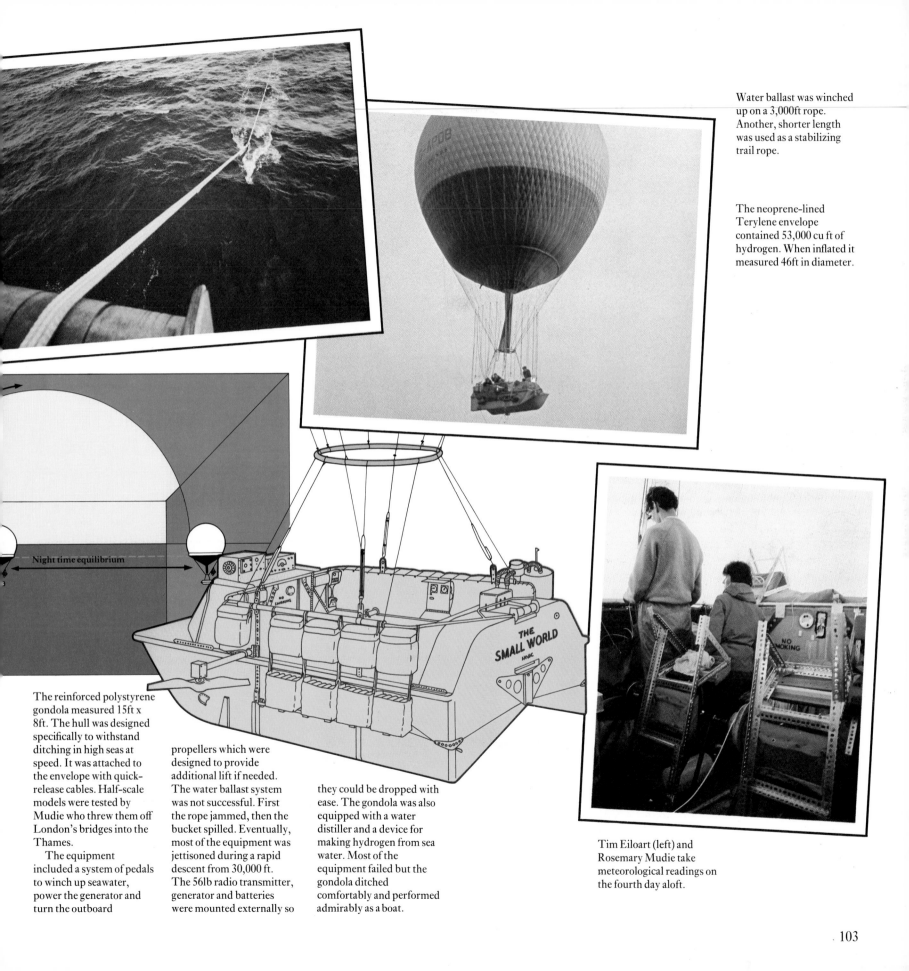

Water ballast was winched up on a 3,000ft rope. Another, shorter length was used as a stabilizing trail rope.

The neoprene-lined Terylene envelope contained 53,000 cu ft of hydrogen. When inflated it measured 46ft in diameter.

Night time equilibrium

THE SMALL WORLD

The reinforced polystyrene gondola measured 15ft x 8ft. The hull was designed specifically to withstand ditching in high seas at speed. It was attached to the envelope with quick-release cables. Half-scale models were tested by Mudie who threw them off London's bridges into the Thames.

The equipment included a system of pedals to winch up seawater, power the generator and turn the outboard propellers which were designed to provide additional lift if needed. The water ballast system was not successful. First the rope jammed, then the bucket spilled. Eventually, most of the equipment was jettisoned during a rapid descent from 30,000 ft. The 56lb radio transmitter, generator and batteries were mounted externally so they could be dropped with ease. The gondola was also equipped with a water distiller and a device for making hydrogen from sea water. Most of the equipment failed but the gondola ditched comfortably and performed admirably as a boat.

Tim Eiloart (left) and Rosemary Mudie take meteorological readings on the fourth day aloft.

Free Life
September 20, 1970

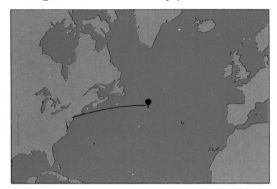

In 1970 Malcolm Brighton, the veteran English balloon pioneer, teamed up with an American couple named Anderson to attempt a west–east crossing. The flight anticipated later methods as it was the first example of a combined hot-air and helium balloon (built by Mark Semich of Semco Balloons). They took off on September 20 and ditched 30 hours later in a storm off Newfoundland. All three people aboard died. No wreckage was ever located.

Yankee Zephyr
August 7, 1973

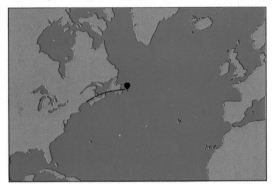

On August 7, 1973, Bobby Sparks set off in *Yankee Zephyr*, another balloon operating on the hot-air/helium combination, and featuring a gondola based on that of *Small World*. It was the first attempt from Bar Harbor, Maine. The flight was terminated by a violent storm after 23 hours. Sparks was rescued.

Light Heart
February 18, 1974

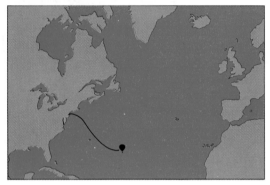

The first 'jet stream' attempt was made by Thomas Gatch in *Light Heart*, a cluster of 10 super-pressure helium balloons built by Raven. The theory followed ideas originating from those of John Wise and should have worked because the balloons used were well tried and tested in carrying scientific payloads for long periods. But Gatch crashed into the ocean and no wreckage was ever found.

Windborne
January 6, 1975

Malcom Forbes mustered a formidable combination of design, planning and money for the second high altitude attempt, in January 1975. But the weather-gods were not impressed. *Windborne* became uncontrollable at take-off and the cluster of helium-filled balloons was cut loose to save the pilots' lives.

Odyssey
August 21, 1975

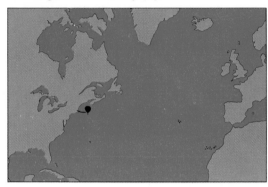

Undeterred by his first failure, Bobby Sparks lifted off in the Semich-built *Odyssey* on August 21, 1975. He was accompanied by a stowaway—his chief ground crewman—adding unexpected weight to the balloon. The flight lasted only 2 hours 5 minutes before Sparks was again in the ocean.

Spirit of '76
June 25, 1976

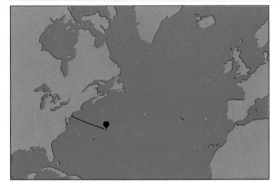

Karl Thomas, part-financier of the Sparks' flight, recovered *Odyssey's* gondola as return on a loan given to the unsuccessful venture. The refitted gondola, attached to the fourth Semich-built envelope to make the Atlantic attempt, lifted off on June 25, 1976, from Lakehurst, New Jersey, the old airship base. *Spirit of '76* was forced down by a storm 550 miles later and Thomas was rescued by a Russian trawler.

Double Eagle
September 9, 1977

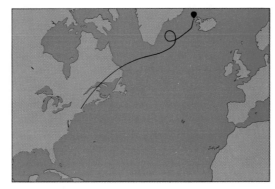

The first sortie by Maxie Anderson and Ben Abruzzo, two pilots from New Mexico, ended in near disaster when they ditched into a stormy ocean off Iceland. They had flown *Double Eagle*—another Yost-built craft—for 64 hours and 2,950 miles. Such a lucky survival should have convinced them to give up, but they were to try again.

Silver Fox
October 5, 1976

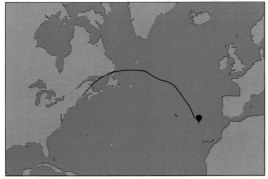

If seven is a lucky number then it didn't quite live up to its promise for Ed Yost, who made the seventh modern attack on the Atlantic. *Silver Fox* was the first Yost-built balloon to make the attempt and I well remember tracking the flight from radio reports along with hundreds of other balloonists at the Albuquerque Fiesta. Yost lifted off on October 5, 1976, smashed all the records set 18 years before by *Small World*, and his course seemed set fair for Europe. Bad luck and a change in the wind direction brought this man, one of the inventors of the modern hot-air balloon, down in mid-ocean some 700 miles from Europe. His new distance record was 2,474 miles.

Eagle
October 10, 1977

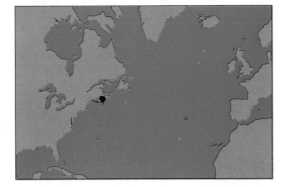

The third Yost-built envelope to be used on a crossing attempt lifted off from Bar Harbor, Maine, on October 10, 1977. The 86,000 cu ft balloon piloted by Reinhard and Stevenson covered a mere 220 miles in 46 hours before crashing in yet another storm.

Accounts of attempted balloon crossings often end with the phrase 'terminated by a violent storm'. It is a loaded phrase but one which cannot convey the drama and the terror experienced by a crew.

I shall never forget Bobby Sparks' description of his flight in *Yankee Zephyr*. Everything had proceeded so peacefully from take-off that he was lulled into a false sense of security and calmly set his alarm clock as he settled in for a sleep. After Sparks failed to report his position at a predetermined time, attempts were made to contact him by radio but the pioneer slept on, oblivious to the fast-approaching horror. He was finally awakened as the balloon gondola pitched violently in the wet, cold reality of a full-blown cumulonimbus cloud. Rain-water was pouring off the envelope in sheets, and fast flooding his unprotected gondola. Icy winds whistled past, freezing him rigid. For minutes he lay numbed by the cold, only vaguely aware that he was near to drowning in the bottom of the boat. The altimeter swept past 5,000, 10,000, 20,000 ft— far higher than his balloon was supposed to fly. He desperately vented gas to halt the climb before *Yankee Zephyr* exploded. The power of the dark cloud sent the balloon racing downward, on a flight path which showed up like a crazy gymnastic exercise on the barograph trace.

Bailing frantically, Sparks tried to keep pace with the influx of water while the balloon continued its pell-mell seaward plunge, stopped feet over the water then raced back into the sky, drawn upward by invisible forces of the atmosphere.

As if once had not been sufficient he was trapped in another vicious cycle of winds until, exhausted and terrified, Sparks heard breaking waves below him and pulled his rip line to send the gondola crashing into the mountainous seas.

Bobby Sparks' tale is tall—but he has the barograph trace to prove it.

Every aspirant so far had been defeated by the weather; but weather was also to be the source of success. Judicious use of westerly winds in combination with a high pressure ridge was the answer—and by 1978 they could be found, and balloons related to them, by satellite forecasting and tracking techniques.

That year two teams were preparing, on opposite sides of the Atlantic, to answer the Great Challenge.

Although the two balloons used helium as a lifting medium, similarities ended there; and, as if in repeat of the technology race of 1783, one team favoured hot air as a means of ballast whereas the other favoured outright lift and a method of moderating solar gain and heat loss.

The British balloonist Don Cameron had, for a long time, aspired to be first across the Atlantic. His Zanussi balloon was designed on the first principle: the helium gas providing the essential lift was surrounded by a cocoon of hot air on much the same principle as the Semich balloons used on previous attempts. After minimal pre-flight trials in Britain, Cameron and Chris Davey travelled to St. John's, Newfoundland, for the take-off. On Wednesday, July 26, at 7.20 local time, they lifted off, delayed by illness from using the departure time advised by the weather forecasters, in a balloon which was unproved, heading for a landfall farther away than any yet achieved.

At first all went well. The new meteorological forecasting techniques really were giving them reliable information. But on July 27 the untested inner (helium) balloon, about which Cameron was already nervous, gave way at 10,000 ft with the sound of a pistol shot. After an initial panic, the two Britons found that the balloon remained manageable. The flight continued. At home, every news broadcast included the latest update of information on the leaking balloon edging towards Europe. Every hour it was a little closer. Day three and day four passed without drama, but all the time the wind was slowing and turning, and with the balloon not capable of delivering its full potential, hopes began to diminish. On day five, confronted with a cumulo-nimbus storm cloud of the type that had killed the Anderson/Brighton crew and which had forced down *Small World*, then Thomas, Reinhard and Sparks, they made the decision to splash down.

The British attempt was over, foiled by a technical flaw in the balloon which had come tantalizingly close to Europe. Nevertheless a French trawler delivered the pilots to a well-deserved welcome party.

Maxie Anderson, Ben Abruzzo and Larry Newman had been waiting at their base in Maine, anxiously following the British attempt and knowing from satellite weather pictures that the Zanussi balloon might make it. Their new balloon, *Double Eagle II*, was an improved version of the one used on their previous crossing attempt and was the fourth Yost-built craft to confront the Atlantic. Filled only with helium, the envelope was capable of great altitude variation without the need to valve gas. To limit the effects of solar and thermal variation, the top half was coated silver to reflect the sun's energy input, while the base was painted black to absorb the more constant energy from a warm ocean at night. This colour scheme and the design of the gondola were almost identical to those of *Small World*, 20 years earlier. Ejecting 3,250 lb of ballast, they progressed across the Atlantic and across the TV screens of millions. In a 137-hour flight they travelled 3,120 miles and flew over Britain to land only 55 miles short of Lindbergh's French landfall after his transatlantic flight.

When the Atlantic was finally conquered, it was done in seemingly effortless style.

LONO81902-8/19/78-LONDON: Double Eagle 11 ballonist's at news conference at the Hilton Hotel on arrival here from Paris 8/19. L/R; Standing, Major Christopher Davey, of the"Zanussi" balloon attempt which failed last month, Larry Newman, Ben Abruzzo, and Maxie Anderson. L/R; Seated, Shirley Hammack (ground-crew), Sandra Newman, Pat Abruzzo and Patty Anderson. UPI (BALLOON) gb/G.Chu

Our happy landing...
Atlantic balloon hero
talks to the Express

NEW SHOCK FOR RADIATION WORKERS

One in seven hit by atom poison

By Peter Hardy

WALKING ON AIR!

By Patrick Clancy

THE three amazing but not-so-young men in their balloon touched down gently in a Normandy wheatfield last night, instant heroes.

And from Paris later, pilot Ben Abruzzo told me how their record trip across the Atlantic from America ended —

● As we came down the sun was shining and all around were fields, beautiful fields, with thousands of people pouring into them.

With such a big gallery there, we wanted specially to make a good landing. As soon as the gondola touched ground we were surrounded.

My immediate feeling was inward. There was pleasure and satisfaction at finally being back on ground, and relief at arriving safely, but there was also the rather sad feeling that a historical moment was just ending.

Ben Abruzzo, 47, with his partners Max Anderson, 42, and Larry Newman, 31, saw their balloon turn to bits by souvenir hunters after landing near Evreux.

From the wheatfield a French Army helicopter flew them 30 miles to Paris where they had to produce their passports.

Outside the American Ambassador's residence they were reunited with their wives. —Pat Abruzzo, Patty Anderson, and Sandra Newman.

The men were cushioned, unshaven, and dog-tired—but delighting. 'We feel marvellous,' Abruzzo insisted.

He explained: 'We were slightly disappointed we didn't make it to Le Bourget where Charles Lindbergh landed 50 years ago.

'But we were only 50 miles short of our goal, so we did' come 3,000 miles or so in about six days. We set the world record for endurance, the world record for distance and we got into the Atlantic once we put all those years and said 'We feel marvellous.

Crowds thronged the Rue du Faubourg St Honore outside his residence—including half a dozen show-girls wearing little more than a smile.

The 110ft tall helium-filled balloon left Presque Isle,

Maine, near the Canadian border just after last Friday noon. Abruzzo, the oldest and formally broke the ocean record by 'somewhat, might on reaching Le Iran West last night Britain's Alcock and Brown ended the first plane crossing in 1919.

Yesterday, Double Eagle II

Turn to Page 16

RADIATION tests on staff at Aldermaston atom plant have produced a shock finding.

One in seven were found to be suffering from deadly plutonium poisoning—and only a small proportion of the workforce has been tested so far.

It will be months before all the workers at the secret H-bomb factory in Berkshire are screened.

The Defence Ministry said last night it was quite likely that other workers would be found to have higher than acceptable levels of plutonium in their lungs.

Demands for an inquiry into radioactive contamination at the plant were met yesterday by Defence Secretary Fred Mulley.

He announced that an independent review of health and safety standards at the centre is to be carried out by Sir Edward Pochin.

Secret

Sir Edward is a doctor and one of the world's leading experts on the effects of radiation.

His report is expected to take about two months to complete.

The Ministry said it then aimed to make public 'the maximum amount of information relevant to health and safety issues.'

The exact number of staff at Aldermaston went but it is known to be several thousand.

Since January, says the firm, 96 of them have been screened.

Twelve of them—including three women laundry workers—have already been told they have up to five times the permitted level of the plutonium in their lungs.

All 12 continue to work at Aldermaston but in non-risk areas.

AT WINDSCALE nuclear plant in Cumbria, 11 workers have been hit by plutonium poisoning, it was revealed last night.

We've done it! Larry Newman, Max Anderson and Ben Abruzzo after touch-down

WHAT A RIP-OFF OF A WELCOME! CENTRE PAGES

High Alpine flying

'...an atmospheric current of extreme velocity took them above the sunny mountains.'

Jules Verne, Five Weeks in a Balloon.

Alpine flying provides unrivalled views of clean mountain landscape; but in return it demands more of a balloonist's skill and courage than any other type of inland flying. It is a dangerous sport for experienced pilots.

The picture postcard view of snowy Alpine peaks as a background to flower-strewn pastures and wooden chalets is real enough, but balloonists see the picture from a different angle. The white-capped peaks which stand protectively above the cosy valleys create severe turbulence. On the windward side a balloon pilot risks being blown hard against the rock faces. On the lee side there is often dramatic curlover with enormous waves of air tumbling down, threatening to punch the air out of the envelope. Over the top of the mountains are found clouds, freezing mist, mountain wave and other ethereal delights not mentioned in the tourist guides.

Alpine topography, in addition to establishing the weather pattern, limits the choice of landing sites. There is no point landing in a field if the only access is a narrow, winding footpath. Pine trees obscure the high slopes and interesting thermic conditions are created as surface temperatures vary from frozen snow to warmer pineneedles. (Winter temperatures reach –30°C.)

Valley bottoms are predictably cluttered. Most of Europe's major rivers have their source in the Alps and streams run everywhere. All the communications lifelines follow the path of the rivers. Roads, railways, overhead cables and chalets occupy the space below a narrow strip of pasture at the bottom of the tree line. Additional hazards are presented by ski lifts, of which there are some 1,500 in Switzerland alone. Landing decisions therefore have to be positive and swift.

Although gas balloons with the long-range ability to float out of mountain country have been flying over the Alps since the eighteenth century, the first big rally was held as recently as 1962 at Mürren.

In the early 1970s, when men like Kurt

For the fliers, the Rhône valley, foggy beneath but craggy and white from the air, is within soaring distance of picturesque postcard chalets.

Ruenzi and Jo Starkbaum were pioneering hot-air mountain flying, it was reckoned by many to be a foolhardy sport since hot-air balloons are more likely to come down in similar conditions to the ones they left. But gradually individual flights became small meetings. And the meetings became bigger. There are now regular meets in Austria, at Zell Am See and Filzmoos, and in Switzerland at Flims and Mürren. One of the biggest and most flamboyant meetings of all is at Chateau d'Oex in Switzerland, a winter competition to which balloonists come in their dozens to fly over some of the most spectacular mountain scenery in the world. On ascension from the Chateau d'Oex launch site, Mont Blanc, at 15,771 ft the highest Alpine peak, and the Eiger are visible.

My own interest in mountain flying was aroused when I heard a 'traditional' English balloonist describing the maniacal flying of an Austrian at a meeting in Flims. Then in 1976 I participated in an event at Zell Am See. The flying scared me half to death when, on my first attempt, I was carried too far with too little fuel on to the shoulders of the Gross Glockner glacier. The fright I received was not quickly

From the take-off site at Chateau d'Oex, a village with its own balloon, a French pilot in *ab's d'absorba* prepares to hop over Mont Blanc to land in Chamonix.

109

forgotten and tempered my approach to the next event I attended, the BP-Polar race in January, 1979. My balloon was Thunder's latest model 77Z, a lightweight machine capable of withstanding Alpine turbulence and fully equipped with skirt, thermistors and double burner.

I carried one crew man and a complete inventory of survival equipment: snow shovel, sleeping bags, bivouac tent, food, heater, ice pick, ropes, flares, stroboscopic distress lights, first-aid kit (including morphine), oxygen and two ASH 360 aircraft radios. If my balloon was going to be speared on one of the peaks I was determined to be rescued alive.

The object of the races was maximum distance, and in the first race our small craft was outclassed by the bigger balloons. Starkbaum won the race with 110 miles. I was fourth at 52 miles, splitting the field. On the second day I flew out across northern Austria and into Germany, winning the race.

The third and last flight was truly Alpine. It was a warmer day (-10°C at 10,000 ft) and I was flying solo, much closer to the peaks than before. Close enough to see the snow powder blowing in plumes off the leeward side of ridges; close enough to find mountain wave taking the balloon gently down at 1,500 fpm and up at the same rate. Close enough to hear my shouts ring back from the rock faces, almost without delay. The views across the isolated mountain tops are best appreciated from a balloon. Mountaineers have too limited a viewpoint, aircraft pilots too little time to appreciate the scale and the detail of the mountain-scape.

By the northern end of the mountains my plan was to go high to find the forecast westerly wind. I could see Austria to my right, swathed in deep cloud. As I climbed, I entered Tauern military airspace but my radio batteries were too weak, after three days of use, to make contact with the controllers. An unseen jet roared past, turned and came back. I cringed in my basket, knocked momentarily off balance by this sudden and violent intrusion.

The winds were not as strong as forecast. I drifted slowly over a high icefield—an inhospitable place to be in a light wind with a depleted fuel supply. The radio was soon totally dead and I could not contact any of the other, now distant, balloons for information on the winds. I looked down at the icefield and north to the swirling fog.

I had to go down. I aimed at a small promontory standing clear of the cloud.

My descent took me west over the Attersee, a lake beneath the clouds, on a course I determined only by the surrounding mountains. With 30 minutes of fuel remaining I found a gentle wind at 6,000 ft, blowing to the north east, taking me back over land which I could not see. Down I went into the enveloping haze of frozen cloud. Looking up, I could see the sun shining through a thin mantle of crystals, creating a rainbow halo above the balloon.

The crown temperature fell, sending the balloon into a cycle of unstable movement, rushing down, stopping and rising again until, as the mists cleared, the balloon steadied and lowered me into a sunny, snow-covered valley.

I flew from side to side, sweeping up the valley, over trees, rivers, powerlines and houses, without ever reaching an open space. At the far end I was thankful to see my retrieve crew and more pleased to notice a small open field for which I aimed. In the chaos of landing among dozens of excited villagers the balloon was torn, but that was of little concern. I was down, back in touch.

With a remote camera Jerry Young photographs himself and Dick Wirth (top left) at 1,200 ft over the Col de Mosses.

Alpine winters (left) mean morning skies of deepest blue and abnormally low ground temperatures.

J&B and *Big Red* head southeast through clear skies towards the Rhône valley. Another balloon is visible far below. Beneath the timber line snow-covered Alpine meadows (left) make good landing sites, when they are accessible to retrieve crews.

Desert delights

A personal dream of flying the first balloon over the Pyramids.

Visibility was down to five yards. The mist swirled round us, leaving our hair a mass of silver droplets and we shivered as we thought of warmer places. We had expected this spot to be as warm as it was exotic, but no. On top of the Great Pyramid of Cheops the weather was foul. Yet another day of frustration, the ninth in succession; so far I had spent only 25 minutes in the air over Egypt, and was no nearer to fulfilling a personal dream of flying across the Pyramids.

The commercial objective was to fly the Pepsi balloon down the Nile and have it photographed against the riverside hotels—Hilton, Sheraton, Meridian and Shepheard's.

But one thing had gone wrong after another. First, by unhappy chance, we had planned to stage our flight on the day of the Feast of the Ghottas, the day, we now discovered, when all Coptic Christians in Egypt pray for rain—with apparent success as the day is renowned for its persistently high rainfall. An alarming weather forecast of thunderstorms, high winds and rain, which seemed to confirm the expectations, had led us to cancel the flight, and so our frustration can be imagined when the day dawned cloudless and perfect for flying.

It was too late for the complicated logistics of rounding up the Pepsi special events team, the press, the movie men, the helicopter pilot and all the other people needed to stage the flight. A difficult operation anywhere; in Cairo the telephone system rendered it unthinkable.

Two short and tricky preliminary flights in turbulent conditions had failed to yield any photographic results as, one after another, the chase cars carrying cameramen got bogged in the treacherous desert sand.

After days of preparation we were becoming Egyptianized and impervious to disaster. On the second possible flight day we organized an event timetable and brooked no changes. It worked. At 1.45 pm we were ready for take-off with gas tanks which had been pre-heated to a pressure of 180 psi on the cooking range of the Pyramids' restaurant, while the chef skilfully manoeuvred

lunchtime steaks around them.

We inflated on a scrubby football pitch under the glare of NBC television lights. At 1.53 pm I lifted off to the cheers of the ragged Cairo urchins come to witness this strange machine. Seven minutes ahead of schedule, I was on course for the flight of a lifetime, realizing a dream I had held since my first visit to Cairo five years before. The main problem I had anticipated was that the wind would be too far right, causing the balloon to be swept westwards and miss the city. As I edged into the sky it was apparent that the opposite was true – the local wind was carrying me relentlessly left, towards Old Cairo, away from the Nile. Desperately I climbed to 1,000 ft, my agreed ceiling for the flight, and still the wind was not 'right'. Now there was little time in which to correct my course and I contacted Cairo Tower to request clearance to 2,000 ft. It was refused. Local air traffic was 'too dense'.

I looked around through the hazy atmosphere and the only aircraft within sight was our noisy Alouette helicopter. Had I really come 3,000 miles, planned for five years, and spent 10 days of frustration for this? Desperate measures were called for. 'Cairo Tower this is *007*. I have a technical problem and am climbing to 2,000 ft. Please alert aircraft in the vicinity'. Silence and clear disbelief. 'Roger, *007*, confirm your altitude at 2,000 ft'. '2,000 ft, over and out'. My technical problem was solved. Slowly but surely I gained right until suspended over the Nile. Now it was time to go down.

The balloon levelled out at 100 ft above the Nile, floating past the Hilton, with my wife Mo waving excitedly on the roof. Then out over the water, crowded with native feluccas, towards the Meridian in the steady northerly breeze. I swept majestically past the corner of the hotel close enough, almost, to shake hands with the spectators crowding on the roof.

Ahead now lay the old pyramids at Saqqâra. Fine judgement brought me in on a descent path which took me directly over the massive stone monuments. The balloon passed within scraping distance of the pyramid walls in its final descent, before slamming down into the sands of the Sahara. Suddenly the desert was alive with movement. Children, old men, camels, donkeys and horses milled around, intrigued but apprehensive, having witnessed a scene which is unlikely ever to be repeated.

It was night by the time the chase crew arrived to help us pack the balloon and carry it back through the moonlit mounds of the desert. But we had done it. The first balloon flight in Egypt. The first flight over the Giza pyramids, and the first flight over Cairo. A total of one week's recce trip, 11 days' hard slog and a mere 100 minutes in the air. It was without reservation worth it!

The desert sand is bumpy and much harder than it looks from the air. After a landing approach was made between the two pyramids of Saqqâra, the balloon was dragged over several dunes.

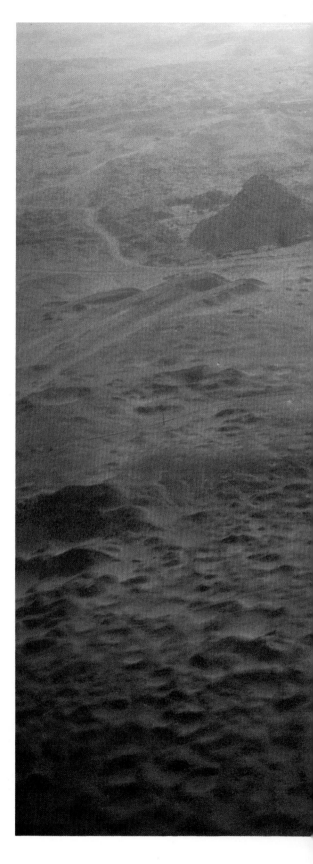

Hot air in the Arctic Circle

The brief was clear: take-off, land, dig in.

'If you have to spend the night in the snow', they explained, 'then it's best to build an igloo.'

The prospect of being stranded was a very real one to most of the balloonists gathered in northern Sweden in the spring of 1977. In keeping with the balloonists' penchant for claiming firsts, a Swedish club had organized the world's first Arctic meet, and several southerners, like myself, had been enticed along. The location for the flight was Kiruna, Sweden's northernmost city, 200 miles inside the Arctic Circle.

Flying conditions were as reasonable as could be expected in temperatures of -25°C. The sky, when clear, was deep blue and calm—at other times grey and filled with swirling snowflakes. The ground was covered in thick snow which, although it would cushion landings, was bound to provide great difficulties for the retrieve crew who, like many people in this frozen wasteland, were driving skidoos or snow scooters.

It was soon apparent that our hosts were not joking about the igloo; it would be impossible not to land in snow. On flight day the pilots' morning briefing was short, but it did include the issue of snow shoes, a shovel and a survival kit to every flier. With the equipment came the complete instructions on building an igloo. Blocks of snow should be cut out roughly 1 ft x 1 ft x 2 ft and placed on the surface to freeze. We were assured that the cooling effect of the wind would accelerate this process. The brief seemed only too clear: take off, land, get stranded, dig in.

The first flight, a hare and hounds race, provided our first aerial view of the wooded Lapland country which stretched away monotonously beneath. Far to the west could be seen the mountain barrier containing Norway's northern tip. To the north lay the unwelcoming airspace of the USSR.

After a short, 30-minute flight the hare balloon dived purposefully into a clearing in the scrubby forest over which we were floating. I was first in a group of five balloons to follow it down. The landing was soft with no bumping and no drag, but to my consternation I realized that the short scrubby pines were actually just the tips of deeply submerged trees.

The cover was so deep that even with snow shoes it was difficult to walk. My passenger made an attempt to reconnoitre but he had to return, exhausted, having failed to reach even the nearest balloon only 150 yds away. We were obviously stranded and could do nothing but wait for the snow scooter patrols manned by members of the Kiruna Motor Club. But we had neither heard nor seen a trace of these loud and brightly painted vehicles since entering the forest.

Our early good humour gave way to anxiety after about an hour of silence. Darkness was not far off. The snow boots and stuffed polyester anoraks which kept us warm against the English winter were proving as useful as paper raincoats. Each small chink in our protective layering let through piercing blasts of cold. A scarf I was wearing cracked when I moved, having been frozen by the wind. After two hours we had dug holes in the snow to shelter from the wind but not an igloo. We could not believe we were going to be left there abandoned after such a short flight.

The first sound of motors provided a boost to our spirits. It was not a snow scooter but a helicopter which hovered above us so that the photographers could get their exposures and then off it flew. We wisecracked about headline stories in the newspapers like those telling of Andrée's disappearance in the Arctic 80 years before.

Then the snow started, cutting visibility and blocking out all sound. We no longer had any contact with the other balloonists close by, but we presumed that they, like us, would be starting to worry. The light was fading fast now, and at last we heard the grinding noise of a skidoo. The crew had not come for us, however, but were looking for Don Cameron who had summoned help on his radio.

We began to build the igloo. At first we did it for exercise to keep warm and occupied, but soon it became a matter of self-preservation. If one stopped working, the perspiration chilled quickly and a layer of ice formed under the clothes. The igloo grew slowly under the rapidly darkening sky.

As we worked, we evolved a simple plan for survival, which was to use the remaining propane to heat ourselves while sheltering from the wind behind the half-finished igloo. We had not left ourselves enough time to complete the structure before darkness fell and today I am under no illusions—if we had stayed there, we would have died. A half-built igloo is useless.

When the headlight beams and the roar of the Yamaha-engined skidoo did at last cut through the trees we were ready to be rescued.

The rescuers arrived with Cameron aboard the sledge, suffering from the cold. Huddled together for mutual warmth under the protection of the tarpaulin, we grumbled all the way back to the hotel. But after a traditional sauna complete with snow dip, followed by a meal, beers and sleep, we were ready for more.

Needless to say, the flights on the following days were shorter and the landings took place closer to the roads than the deceptively cosy-looking forests.

The biggest effect of cold weather on flying equipment is in the variation of fuel pressure. On a warm day typical pressure would be 80–140 psi. On a cold day this can drop to as little as 25 psi. The difference in power output from the burner is critical, especially to competition pilots. Two ways of stabilizing fuel pressure are to artificially pressurize the propane with nitrogen or, more simply, to use pre-heated tanks with good insulation.

Bruce Comstock, 1979 US Champion and a man with experience of hard Michigan winters, effectively demonstrated the advantages of pre-heated fuel during that year's world championship meeting in Uppsala, Sweden, where the ambient temperatures were around -20°C. Every morning Bruce could be seen sitting in his van with a portable generator humming at full output, powering the electric blanket around his tanks. He was the only pilot not to experience severe freezing problems.

Skidoos of the local motor club compacted the snow on the launch field so that competitors in a hare and hounds race could take off. On this occasion Dick Wirth was the hare.

Chariot of the gods

Was the secret of flight known 2,000 years ago?

In his book *Chariots of the Gods*, Erich von Daniken postulates that the mysterious markings across the Peruvian Nazca Plain were laid out as landing sites by previous visitors to this planet. This is probably the best-known of the many theories on the origins and purpose of these massive designs which cover over 200 square miles of desert. Made up of long lines of piled stones, the markings form patterns which can be seen only from the air.

Researchers backed by the International Explorers Society agreed with von Daniken that the designers must have been capable of flight, but on the type of chariot used their opinion differed. They believed that people of the Nazca civilization, of over 2,000 years ago, had made and flown hot-air balloons and their aim was to prove it.

The main evidence, a piece of pottery in Lima, bears a design which is unmistakably that of a balloon, but there is more historical justification for believing that hot-air flight was known in South America. After all, Bartolomeu de Gusmao had gone from Brazil to Portugal to show his balloon years before Montgolfier.

Using materials which would have been available to the pre-Incan Nazca people, the team based its 1975 design on the simple, one-piece tetrahedral shape shown on the pottery. This shape represents the most simple way to fold an uncut piece of material. The envelope was sewn as one spiral gore by Raven Industries in South Dakota. The reed gondola, which resembled Thor Heyerdahl's boat *Ra*, was made by Indians at Lake Titticaca.

The British balloonist Julian Nott was invited to pilot the *Condor I*. His co-pilot was to be Jim Woodman and the crew consisted of more than 20 specialists—Raven technicians, back-up pilots, archaeologists and most importantly, Doc Crane, an American smoke balloonist whose talents were called on during the inflation.

The material was too porous to be inflated with anything other than smoke, so Crane dug a trench to contain the tar-burning fire over which the envelope would be held. After many hours and some small outbreaks of fire, the smoke

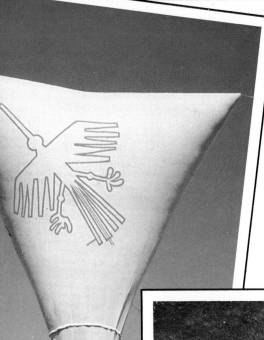

sealed the porous fabric and gave shape to the 80,000 cu ft balloon.

On arrival in the region the team had noticed that on most days there was absolutely no wind, a factor which helped to sway the minds of the many sceptics, and mollify the apprehensive pilots.

Nott and Woodman, both tall men, rose easily into the sky, sitting astride the reed gondola which had been made to the scale of the diminutive Peruvian Indians. *Condor I* was up to its task, however, and it took the two to a height of about 300 ft. From this position the fliers looked around and realized that they had ascended from the centre of a large triangular design which they had not noticed from the ground. The balloon had no vents or flying controls, so after a few minutes ballast had to be ejected as the balloon began a fast descent.

On touching down, the two aeronauts stepped out of the gondola and let *Condor I* fly off on it own, providing them with a replay of what the large crowd had seen. The balloon rose handsomely to about 1,700 ft and came down undamaged some 20 minutes later.

The expedition had proved that balloons could have been made and flown in that area in ancient times. The results satisfied Peruvian authorities that the stone lines should be protected monuments. The short flight had been a complete success but no one was any wiser as to the meaning of the great designs. Studies continue.

The designs painted on *Condor I* are versions of those on the desert floor which can only be seen from the air.

Smokies

The Montgolfiers were right— 'phlogiston' can be used to lift people off the ground. Smoke-filled bags have been carrying people aloft since long before the days of the hot-air revival, but their flights are short, spectacularly uncontrollable and one-way only. A world apart from any other aeronautical activity are the barnstorming 'balloon men', who fly and jump from their 'smokies' at state fairs, carnivals and air shows across America.

Made of muslin, or other porous cloth, the balloons are filled with hot air and smoke from kerosene burners, while supported on poles. Once the smoke has sealed the cloth and inflated the envelope, the pilot is strapped into a harness, the tether rope is cut and the smokie rises straight up, bucking and swaying at first, then climbing more sedately until it stops and hangs in the air at around 1,000 ft. When he reaches the zenith of his flight the daredevil balloon man jumps and descends by parachute. The balloon turns upside down, empties through the neck, and falls back to be reclaimed and used again.

The greatest exponents of this show-business tradition were W.H. Donaldson whose performances enlivened the Civil War era, and Captain Eddie Allen. Allen is now recognized by balloonists as a heroic descendant of Garnerin and he is frequently invited to speak at balloon club dinners. The captain is no longer an active jumper but he has passed his knowledge on to Doc Crane, who makes his own balloons and assisted at Nazca.

The smokie act is a crowd-pleaser, but not one which many aeronauts try to emulate, especially when they see the primitive equipment used. As well as being a stunt it is a reminder of what may have been the first flying machine.

119

Flying over from Dover

The illusion of being becalmed can mesmerize a pilot.

Crossing the English Channel was one of the first ballooning adventures and it remains a challenge to this day. To the best of my knowledge the water has only been crossed from France to England on one occasion — during the 1906 Gordon Bennett race, when an uncommon south-westerly wind was blowing. The trip from England to France has been made more often since Ed Yost and Don Piccard paved the hot-air way in 1963.

The obvious difficulties of flying over any body of water are compounded by the shape of the Channel. The juxtaposition of the opposite coasts, which are only 20 miles apart at the narrowest point, is not compatible with the wind which usually flows up the Channel rather than across it. Even when pilots have waited for a favourable wind, the slightest shift in direction will swing a balloon too far from land. In 1963 Yost landed near Belgium, close to the northern limit. A team of women who flew in 1979 ended up at Le Touquet, close to the southernmost landfall.

The tradition of Channel crossings covers a spectrum from bizarre bathtub races to £50,000 aviation challenges. One of the most adventurous stunts took place on July 21, 1977. Three balloons were piloted by Phillip Hutchins, who had flown the Channel before, David Liddiard and myself. The difference between this and previous flights was that we all carried oxygen, I carried a cameraman, and Phillip and David carried two hang-glider pilots, Ken Messenger and Brian Milton, strung below their baskets.

The idea was simple. The balloons were to climb to over 13,000 ft above Dover (hence the oxygen) and release the gliders which would then head for France. We took off at dawn and rose slowly, so as not to upset the suspended birdmen. Above the morning mist in the clear blue sky at 13,000 ft, Milton was the first to let go. The cameraman tried to record his release but the glider fell away so fast that he could not keep it in his sights. Milton was not heading in the right direction either, for he flashed past beneath us almost parallel with the English coast

and only later turned eastwards over the sea.

Messenger hung on until he reached 18,000 ft, then cut loose and went streaking down towards France at a speed later estimated to be over 60 mph. Ken made it to the other side, as did the balloons, but by that time Brian was still miles from the coast, smack in the middle of the shipping lanes, swimming for his life. The dramatic ending to his flight had been half-expected but he was lucky to be spotted in the water and picked up by a Russian trawler.

The following year the Hot-Air Balloon Company staged a hare and hounds race across the Channel. After an aborted first attempt, the hare pilot, world altitude record holder Julian Nott, took off in *Jumpin' Jack*, the first-ever Thunder balloon, to be followed by Phillip Hutchins and three others.

The race was won by Hutchins who landed at Cap Griz Nez at 7.00 am after a 90-minute flight. Paul Keene was last in the Osram light bulb balloon, but he landed with a story to tell. While flying at 100 ft he had passed over a supertanker, along the deck of which a crewman was cycling peacefully. When he looked up there was a giant light bulb floating over the waves. The sailor fell off the bike in amazement and lay, sprawled on the deck, too shocked to return the pilot's wave.

Crossing large expanses of water can be unnerving for pilots because there is no perception of speed. The balloon, which moves with the wind and therefore at the same speed as the waves, often appears to have stopped. A casual glance down can be disturbing and on a long flight this illusion can mesmerize a pilot. While making the first crossing of the North Sea in 1979, Simon Faithfull and Peter Morgan almost succumbed to the illusion that they were becalmed, but on reaching the coastline their panic increased when they noticed from the bend of the trees that the ground wind speed was actually over 35 mph. Tom Donnelly felt the same fear of being becalmed without fuel when he crossed from the Isle of Man to England.

Insurance companies specifically exclude balloonists from flying over large bodies of water—but, as if in declaration of their freedom, balloon pilots resist all attempts to restrain them. They will continue to make difficult flights for their own satisfaction, and one of the most appropriate flights for a British pilot is the cross-Channel trip to France.

A practice launch session before the cross-Channel hang-glider event (top). In 1978 the six-year-old *Jumpin' Jack* was the hare balloon. *Osram* came in last.

Big game ballooning

You can almost scratch the animals' backs.

The hippos were lumbering noisily among the tents at the Governor's Camp in the heart of Kenya's Masai Mara game reserve. I had spent a restless night while a herd of elephant tramped around my tent but now I was being roused from my semi-sleep. It was 6 am and time to start the flying day in one of the most far-out of all flying businesses.

The crew, who had risen several hours before the flight, were boiling the fuel tanks to produce sufficient pressure while the cooks prepared the 'bush breakfasts'.

The Masai Mara, an extension of the Serengeti game park, is a marvellous place to fly. The winds blow constantly from north to south at the same pace from July to March. Two companies take advantage of this stable climate to provide a regular air safari service over the bush. Air Libre operates three balloons which take off each morning between 6.30 and 7.00, carrying four or five passengers each. The 1980 prices are about $200 per head for flight and champagne breakfast. Such an experience cannot come cheap.

This is a superb way to see game. The animals are rarely frightened by the balloon and the passengers are able to take snaps of everything that moves. When one is flying gently in the tangy fresh air, free from the dust and bumpiness of a jeep safari, the scene is viewed with a degree of intimacy not possible from the ground.

Soon after take-off we were drifting low down the River Mara over the gaping pink jaws of enormous hippos. Cranes broke cover in the bush and a giraffe ran from the noise as I fired the burner to maintain height.

Following the regular morning wind flow, the balloon swung left over Paradise Plain to bring us in view of our first killing—a pack of hyena bringing down a wildebeest. The prey had no chance, but at least the kill was quick and efficient.

The rays of the morning sun bathed the bush in a golden glow. Shadows began to appear and more animals became recognizable in the long grass. All around the air was full of shrieks, whoops and screams of animals, the clatter of breaking trees, and the smell of the bush, indescribably pungent at 500 ft.

In July and August the great herds of wildebeest are migrating; millions of weary animals strung out across the plains, prey to hyena and lion, and victims of suffocation as they try to ford the Mara. From horizon to horizon the plain is filled with their straggling, single-minded trek. By February the scrub grass has grown and flowered. Families of wart-hog scurry through, only the tails visible over the wafting tops. Antelope, zebra and elephant abound in the plains, all witnessed from the secure basket of a balloon swooping just above their heads.

Landing is always the trickiest part of a flight, but there are some features peculiar to Africa.

HIPPOPOTAMUS

Photo by Joseph L. Popp

Copyright: MAN AND NATURE PRESS, Cambridge MA, U.S.A.
Printed by International Aeradio (EA) Ltd., N...

A lion ate our
Nikons, but
apart from that
and inclement
weather all is well
Record flight delayed
a few days so I
will not be back
until the
weekend.
Regards to all
Jerry.

Marshall Editions
71 Eccleston Sq.
London SW1
ENGLAND

The heavily loaded balloons travel fast over acacia trees and hungry animals. The retrieve crew, having raced ahead, wait in the regular landing area as the basket bumps and drags across the grass towards them.

I could hear the *Marseillaise* being sung by the French pilot of the second balloon who swears it takes people's minds off the approaching thorn bushes. Seconds later the passengers tumbled out, their relief at landing safely tempered with a sadness that the safari was over. The champagne flowed and the bush breakfast began.

Of course, things are not always perfect. On one occasion when I was retrieving we had a puncture on our chase jeep and we arrived late, to find the balloon in a remote spot far from the road. By the time one of the sharp-eyed Masai retrieve crew had spotted them, the pilot, with passengers behind his back, was firing the burner at a pack of mangy hyena whose hunger had not been assuaged by the breakfast scraps.

After breakfast the tourists' safari is over, but for the crews the job is only half completed. The balloon has to be packed away and driven back to camp through the long grass, across waterlogged plains, by raft over crocodile and hippo-infested rivers. While the tourists leave the camp with images of the flight on film and in memory, the balloon crews have many more hours of work. The burners are checked and maintained; tanks refilled and cleaned. The landings are rough on the baskets, runners and rawhide edges requiring constant replacement. These are probably the only balloons with real African buffalo and cowhide protection to the wicker. New runners are fashioned from local wood in African style.

Sometimes the envelopes require patching, where they have been caught on thorn bushes or, as on one famous occasion, when a hyena ate through the canvas bag and attacked the nylon inside it. Unaware of the problem we laid out the balloon on the launch site to discover it looking like a moth-eaten rag. There was no flying that day and we had to invent 'bush' style repairs to get into the air.

A basket load of five passengers for the pilot who is squeezed into the far corner. The maximum load for the AX9 balloons is pilot plus seven passengers.

Breakfast time provides tourists with a rare chance to sit in the open. During other types of safari, people must remain in a vehicle.

Flight to freedom

The border guards' lights searched them out.

The Thuringian Forest in East Germany, close to the border with the West, is famous for its romantic beauty and legends, but the tense group of people gathered there in a small clearing on the night of September 15, 1979, were more concerned with creating their own piece of romantic history. They were about to make the awesome, final decision to flee to the West.

The Strelczyk and Wetzel families, four adults and four children, sat listening to the silence of the forest, until satisfied that they were not being observed. Then they began to unpack the small trailer attached to one of their cars, unravelling the 85-ft-long envelope of a home-made hot-air balloon. The multi-coloured balloon, sewn from odd lengths of material, had never been inflated before, but now, by the light of the car headlights, air was fanned in and heated with a burner.

Once the big 108,000 cu ft envelope was 'light', the eight people climbed aboard a 54-inch-square, open platform made of angle-iron and wood. Their awareness of the dangers was heightened by the memory of a similar flight three months previously which had dumped them 200 yds short of the border. This time the wind was more favourable, blowing at 10–15 knots from the north-east, into West Germany.

The children sat facing inwards, with their backs to the propane tanks in each corner of the platform. The adults stood facing out into the darkness, holding the load ropes to keep the mouth of the envelope open. The ragged, yellow flame of the liquid burner, directed through a length of stovepipe, licked up into the envelope, providing the lift to carry the 1,600 lb load.

At 2.40 am, 40 minutes after making the decision to go, they lifted off, brightly illuminated against the night by the glow of the flame. They continued to burn as the only way out was up, and the balloon soon reached 6,500 ft, where it should have been invisible to observers on the ground. They had been spotted at take-off, however, and as the beams of the border guards' lights began to search them out, Peter Strelczyk, the 37-year-old pilot and instigator of the plan, climbed to about 7,900 ft.

After some 20 minutes of flying they estimated that they must be close to the border, but there was

no way of telling. A slow descent was initiated because the fuel was running low when, suddenly, back at 6,500 ft, the burner spluttered on the last gasp of propane and the descent became rapid, sending the balloon spinning down almost out of control. By now the crew were sufficiently acclimatized to the morning light to see that the balloon was moving fast across the German countryside. It skimmed trees, hit a bush and smashed into the ground, lifted briefly and then settled back to a final safe landing. The flight had lasted 30 minutes—but on which side of the border had they touched down?

The men took a reconnaissance trip and spotted a police car, alerted to the unusual goings-on by local residents. The police were West German. The flight to freedom had succeeded. A red flare was sent up as a signal to the wives and children who emerged from their hiding place to indulge in a bout of hysterics— laughing, crying, hugging each other in the joy of being alive and free.

The 1,200 yards of fabric, purchased in small quantities to avoid arousing suspicion, had been sewn by the wives, Doris and Petra, in the basement of the Strelczyk's house in Poessneck.

The refugees later saw their balloon inflated for the first time in daylight. It was handsome, but the equipment horrified balloonists used to normal standards of safety and comfort.

FK-6009 9/17/79 NAILA, West-Germany: Two members of the West German Technical Aid Service stand by the home-made hot air balloon which carried two East German families to freedom across the deadly Iron Curtain frontier near here 9/16. Only one of the balloon's eight passengers suffered slight injuries during the hard landing in total darkness.   hba/   dpa/UPI

Daily Mail

MONDAY, SEPTEMBER 17, 1979   10p

THE FASTEST MAN ON EARTH! CENTRE PAGES

Families escape to West by balloon

UP, UP AND AWAY TO FREEDOM

TWO young families yesterday brought off the most fantastic defection of all—over the East-West German border at 1,500ft. in a home-made hot-air balloon.

Four adults and four children, the youngest only two years old, made a 30-minute flight to freedom clinging to a wooden platform about 4½ft. square.

Above them was the balloon envelope, 137ft. high and 114ft. across, stitched together by the two wives from nylon sheets and curtains.

The platform had a single safety precaution — a clothes rope wound round four corner stanchions. The children were at the corners, one on each post.

The adults hung on to a flimsy cage in the middle which contained four large cylinders of butane gas to power crude hot air burners

Terrified

This was the extraordinary craft that rose into the night sky at 240 a.m. from a remote field outside the East German village of Poessnec, in the province of Thuringia. Six miles to the south lay the border, Bavaria—and freedom. It had taken a nail-biting hour to inflate the balloon.

It was a clear, starlit night and the wind was right. But it was bitterly cold and they were terrified.

At one awful moment during the flight, a searchlight presumably manned by Communist border guards, actually caught the balloon. The escapers waited for the shooting to start—but, inexplicably nothing happened.

They were the more astonished because on a previous attempt in July their balloon had come down 200 yards short of the border. They managed to get away, but the wreckage was found by border guards.

The pilot and the man who designed the balloon, was 37-year-old aircraft mechanic Hans-Peter Strelzik. His friend Gunther Wetzel, a 24-year-old bricklayer, and Strelzik's sons Frank, 15, and Andreas, 11, helped him to build it while the wives sewed. They bought the material bit by bit in different places so as not to attract attention and hid it in a cellar.

They did it, Strelzik said, not because either family was badly off in material terms—'things were pretty good for us over there by East German standards. We each had a house and a car.

'But it was no longer possible for us to lie to our children and put up with the political conditions.'

Yesterday's flight, like the

Turn to Page 2, Col. 2

From COLIN LAWSON in Bonn

The joy that says 'We're free!' The escapers and their balloon yesterday

Revolt of the Labour town halls

By HARVEY ELLIOTT, Home Affairs Reporter

A MASS revolt by town halls against the proposed cuts in public spending now faces the Government.

Thirty - five leaders from Labour-controlled cities are to meet this week to draw up a united campaign of action against the cuts.

Then they will confront Environment Secretary Mr Michael Heseltine and tell him: 'We will not reduce our spending.'

The crunch will come on Thursday when Mr Heseltine is due to speak at the local government conference in Scarborough.

Before that all the Labour leaders of metropolitan authorities will meet to work out how to defy his calls for an immediate 3 per cent reduction in their budgets.

Councils throughout the country have been horrified by the effects of the Government's calls for cuts. Many have openly refused to co-operate.

Disastrous

Even Tory-controlled Oxfordshire, in which Mr Heseltine has his constituency, has said it cannot make the cuts as quickly as he is demanding.

The latest council to join the growing number of rebels is Lambeth, in London.

Its leader, Mr Ted Knight, said last night that the council was refusing to make any cuts at all.

The metropolitan authorities are the big spenders in local government. They represent the biggest cities and conurbations in the country and a mass attack on Government policies by them could have disastrous consequences.

Mr Heseltine is determined to force through his plans not only to cut spending this year but to reduce it by a further 5 per cent next year.

And he has warned the local authority associations that he is prepared to introduce legislation, if necessary.

His obvious course of action however is to starve the rebels of Whitehall cash, forcing them to place the burden of spending on their own ratepayers.

In this way, he believes, local voters would see that the fault lay with their own council and throw them out.

Already some authorities are predicting massive rate increases from next April. In many London boroughs ratepayers could be faced with paying 50 per cent more than now.

INSIDE: Femail 12, 13, Mail Diary 23, TV Guide 26, Prize Crossword 30, Letters, Stars & Strips 34, City 38, Classified Adverts 39-41, 45

The art and the science/Take-off

A British balloonist seeking a country estate would write an advertisement in these terms: 'Well-drained field required, served by a well-paved access road. Must be in a gentle valley, with high trees on the windward side, and situated far west of restricted airspace'.

In theory a balloon can be launched from anywhere; in practice there are topographical, climatic and legalistic considerations that make some places much more promising than others. Balloon crews find choice launch sites that fulfil their requirements and persuade the landowners to give permission for regular flying. A phone call to the owner obtains the go-ahead for a particular day. Crews can then use a familiar assembly point with well-known characteristics.

In the wide open spaces of the United States, where calm weather so often prevails, the property-seeking balloonist might omit the

Out of the van, on with the fan, then fire up the burner.

It can get hot behind the burner—and holding down the crown line is always hard work. A less exhausting role for crew members is pulling out the envelope fabric to stop it being sucked into the flame.

Watching inflations is a spectator sport in Albuquerque—hot-air capital of the world, where mass launches of 200 balloons take place.

Of some consolation to the ground crews (left) is a good view of the departing balloons.

requirement for a barrier of protective trees.

He might also not be so neurotically concerned about 'airspace' as the British balloonist. Britain's wind normally flows to the east, carrying southern balloonists straight into London's airspace – one of the most trafficked and complex flying areas in the world. (They dare not operate east of the city since there's so little space between urban areas and the sea).

In Austria, the problem is turned on its head. The law decrees that a balloon is an aircraft and must behave like one. So Austrian aeronauts launch from the centres of large airfields, and only on very calm days, carrying obligatory radios to communicate with other air traffic. Most balloonists avoid controlled airspace; Austrians are not allowed out of it.

As balloons fly with the weather, and not through it, balloon pilots have considerations which do not affect pilots of conventional aircraft. For instance local ground fog, 50–100 ft thick, would not bother the pilot of a light aircraft intending to land some 200 miles away after a two-hour flight. But it could be critical for a balloonist with a 15-mile flight plan.

Balloon pilots are greatly affected by the speed and direction of the wind; the pilots of aircraft only slightly. The aircraft pilot will make allowances for the wind by calculating a course from A to B which takes account of the amount of drift at an angle to his track. At launch or landing he selects a runway which allows him to face his aircraft into wind and gain lift. The balloon pilot, however, cannot fly from A to B if the wind is flowing in a different direction. He therefore derives his course from the forecast wind direction, selects his approximate flight time and, if he has a desired landing area B, plots a take-off site A. He then uses wind direction changes with altitude to fly from A to B.

More commonly a balloon pilot decides on an approximate flight duration – say 2 hours at 10 knots – and selects his launch site accordingly. He can then give an approximation of B from his knowledge of the prevailing conditions, but will not determine his precise B until well into the flight. This is one of the essential differences between balloon flying and most other forms of aviation. Balloonists seldom have a destination in mind, but are more concerned with enjoying themselves on a magical mystery flight.

Only one fuel tank is used during inflation. The basket is laid on its side and the envelope is connected to the load-carrying structure and spread out over the ground. Two crew members hold open the mouth while a small fan is used to partially inflate the balloon with cold air. Once the burner is turned on the rush of entrained air surging up the envelope tends to draw the mouth closed behind it. A 20,000 cu ft one-man balloon is filled taut within 60 seconds. A large 140,000 cu ft balloon can take 10-15 minutes to inflate.

While the cold inflation is proceeding the pilot enters the envelope to make preliminary pre-flight checks on operational lines, rigging, pulleys, Velcro tabs, flying wires, parachute and envelope fabric.

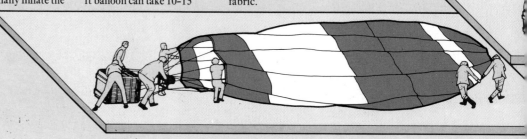

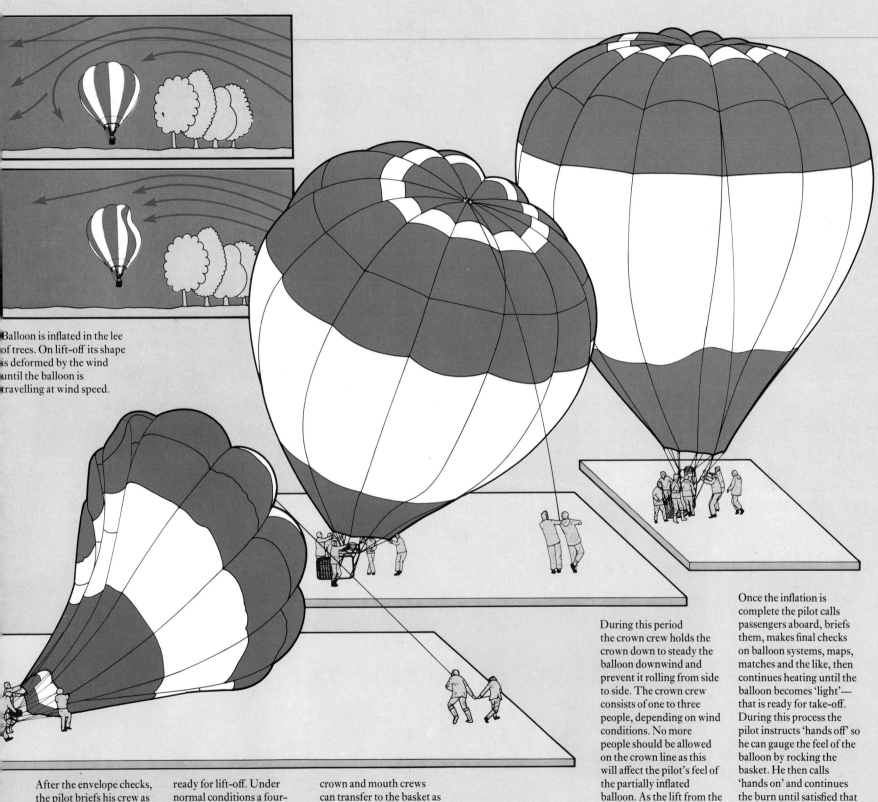

Balloon is inflated in the lee of trees. On lift-off its shape is deformed by the wind until the balloon is travelling at wind speed.

After the envelope checks, the pilot briefs his crew as to their duties during the launch. One to three people hold the basket down until ready for lift-off. Under normal conditions a four-man balloon can be inflated and launched with a crew of four to five people. The crown and mouth crews can transfer to the basket as the envelope fills and rises above the basket.

During this period the crown crew holds the crown down to steady the balloon downwind and prevent it rolling from side to side. The crown crew consists of one to three people, depending on wind conditions. No more people should be allowed on the crown line as this will affect the pilot's feel of the partially inflated balloon. As the lift from the envelope increases, the crew walk the crown line to the basket.

Once the inflation is complete the pilot calls passengers aboard, briefs them, makes final checks on balloon systems, maps, matches and the like, then continues heating until the balloon becomes 'light'— that is ready for take-off. During this process the pilot instructs 'hands off' so he can gauge the feel of the balloon by rocking the basket. He then calls 'hands on' and continues the burn until satisfied that he can take off smoothly and climb clear of any downwind obstructions.

Inflated balloons can huddle close together on the ground when there are lots of willing helpers to hang on to baskets and steady the rolling movements as envelopes collide. In the air, however, balloons must be separated vertically. Massed launches have to be carefully timed to ensure that each balloon has sufficient room to manoeuvre.

Officials in fluorescent jackets oversee the launch procedure. When a pilot is ready to move off he has to wait for their permission. The officials keep account of all balloon activity around the field and only release a pilot when the airspace is free.

Balloons thus appear to pop out of the mass like bubbles from a fizzy drink, but the apparently random order belies the reality.

This typical British launch site (far right) was used for the 1977 cross-Channel race. Although the ground wind was about 12 knots, the trees and raised ground provided shelter for the balloons to stand upright.

Two launches from Castle Howard (centre) where 100ft trees provide cover throughout the day.

At Albuquerque (right) there is no shelter. The 'thin' early morning winds do not affect launches. Balloons are allocated launch sites in rows on an alfalfa field.

Using wind and weather

Day-time-anabatic wind

The effect of solar heating on south-facing mountain sides is commonly felt in the Alps and is particularly dangerous to balloon pilots since there is no way of counteracting it. On calm days one can use it to progress from one valley to the next, but it is usually a menace when attempting to land in a steep valley. If the prevailing wind is at right angles to the valley, landing becomes a problem since there is only a narrow 'chimney' to slide down and land in. It is easy enough to overshoot and if the descent is started too early the thermic updraught forces the balloon back.

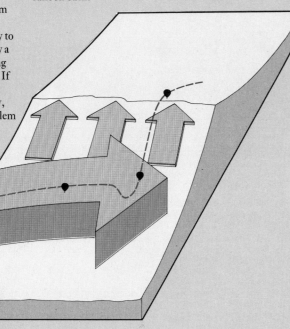

Curlover

Curlover is the commonest form of air turbulence experienced by balloonists. It can vary from a light disturbance behind trees in an evening breeze to severe, shaking downdraughts on the lee side of steep hills and escarpments.

Light curlover is easily counteracted by boosting the balloon's lift with the burner, but severe turbulence can be dangerous and must be avoided where possible. In a way it is akin to a reverse thermal. The turbulent wind flow curls back and deflates the balloon, depriving it of lift and compounding the effect of a general downward movement of the air mass. Curlover is the commonest cause of minor accidents, often forcing low-flying balloons into trees and fences with its unanticipated turbulence.

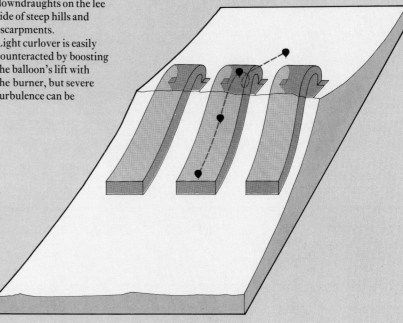

Night-time—katabatic wind

A phenomenon in hilly or mountainous country is katabatic wind which occurs commonly in the evening. Air cools and rolls down the hillside in layers up to 200 ft thick. It is sufficiently powerful to overcome the effects of a light, general wind flow and has forced my balloon out of the sky on more than one occasion. The first time was nearly disastrous and we ended in a large oak tree waiting to be rescued by a passing farmer. Since that time I have been careful to keep the balloon 'hot' and ready to ascend when approaching the side of a hill on a calm evening.

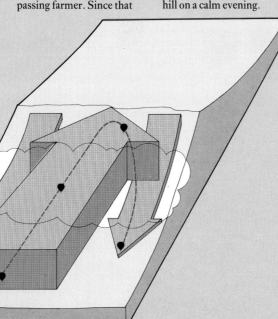

Wave

Glider pilots search out and enjoy the wave effect at great altitude but when balloonists face it at low level it can present a problem. The wind flow is forced into a wave pattern and a balloon in the air mass will oscillate with it. The effect is usually powerful, but as long as equilibrium temperature is maintained it is relatively harmless.

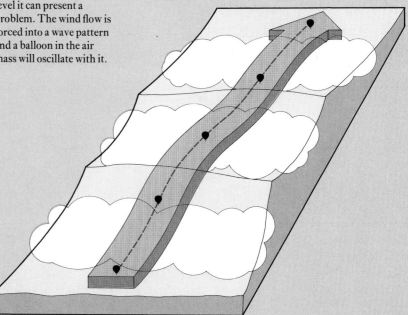

Valley wind

Valley wind is a favourite of all pilots because its usually gentle effects allow one to steer at a considerable angle to the main airflows. In competition a good pilot will gain vital yards, and fun flying is enhanced as one tries to evade pursuing balloons or confuse the retrieve crew by changing direction through as much as 90°. The effect is greater in steep valleys where anabatic and katabatic winds combine to create a soft-centred whirlpool.

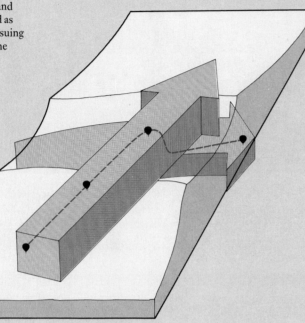

Thermals

Fliers encounter thermals whenever differences in the ground temperature cause differential heating of the air. Sometimes one flies into an existing thermic updraught but often a balloon creates its own thermal by bursting the bubble and breaking the surface tension which is holding it down. Once the hot air is released, it hurls the balloon malevolently upwards. 'Bubbles' of hot air burst around the balloon, causing it to rock and sway in a terrifying manner. Each bubble causes the envelope to cave in as it twists and turns in the turbulence.

Thermals are regarded by balloonists as their biggest enemy, because the only way out is up and it is not uncommon on hot days to be carried up several thousand feet, shaken and buffeted all the way.

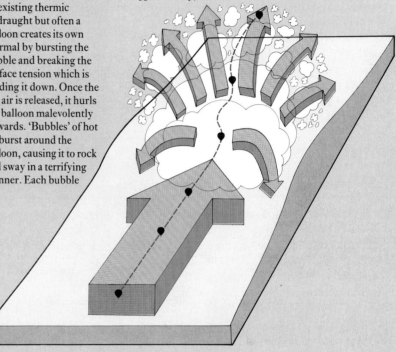

Obstacle flow

Balloonists often discover facts about micro-climate winds and weather which astonish other pilots who do not fly so close to the ground. Low level air currents are powerful and will sweep a balloon over or around hills even though the pilot makes adjustments for changes in altitude. It is easy for two balloons which launch together to become separated by great distances and cross paths again on the far side of an obstacle.

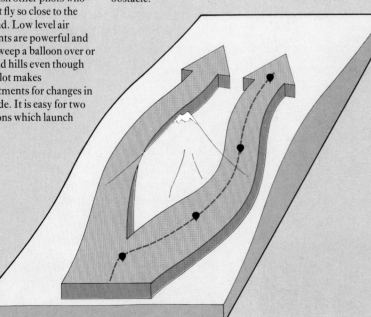

Sea breeze

This is usually a late afternoon and evening effect occurring in coastal areas and near inshore lakes. The 'breeze' or moving air mass is up to 500 ft thick and will accelerate a prevailing wind in the same direction or cause deceleration and moderate turbulence in a contrary prevailing wind.

It can crush the balloon as if it had hit a brick wall, but if used sensibly 180° turns can be made using its power.

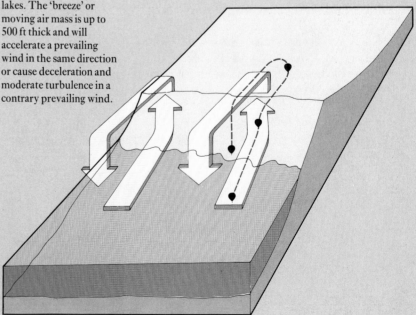

A basic knowledge of meteorology will serve most balloonists well enough. The one question they ask about the weather is 'how flyable is it?'. Ballooning usually takes place in relatively good conditions which are governed more by local micro-climates than the overall weather picture. Most balloonists obtain all their weather information on the morning of the flight from one call to the local met. office, which provides information on the speed and direction of the wind and the cloud cover.

A knowledge of local effects such as sea breeze and valley wind is important. In Britain gusty winds make it difficult to land in small fields; in the wide open spaces of Texas, winds of the same speed are less intimidating. In the Alps local insolation often generates high pressure zones; there may be pilots flying happily in Austria's Inn Valley when others are grounded by heavy storms 100 miles north in Augsburg.

An understanding of synoptic weather forecast charts is helpful, especially to balloon crews who have to drive many miles to a meet. The simplistic presentation of the weather which is used on TV and in the newspapers is easy to interpret and enables the next few hours' weather to be predicted. The main symbols are the isobars—lines which join areas of equal pressure like contours. Cold and warm front symbols show the interfaces between masses of air of different temperatures.

The rotation of the Earth produces an anti-clockwise twist in the northern hemisphere to what would otherwise be a straight wind flow into the low pressure areas. These winds flow parallel to the isobars. Below 1,500–2,000 ft the wind's speed is reduced by friction with the Earth's surface and this drag changes the direction of the wind by approximately 30°, accounting for the ballooning adage—'Right with height'. When the isobars are close the pressure drop is great and the wind speed is high.

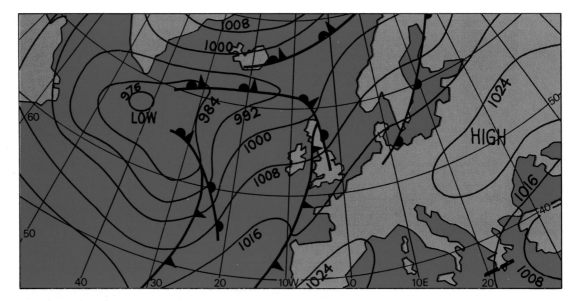

This synoptic chart gives an unhappy forecast for British balloonists. The disintegrating high pressure area creates unstable cold and warm front weather. From northern Spain to Yugoslavia weather conditions are perfect.

A low begins when warm and cold air masses, moving next to one another, produce a decrease in pressure as the warm air intrudes into the cold. This 'atmospheric hole' is then filled by the higher pressure air which surrounds it. Winds are anti-clockwise. If you stand with your back to the wind the centre is to your left. Below the Equator the direction is reversed.

In high pressure areas the winds flow in a clockwise direction, slowly except on the edge of large highs where faster winds are common. In winter the lack of cloud cover allows the Earth to radiate heat and leads to frost. In summer the sun more than makes up for night-time heat loss.

Warm front

Cold front

1024
Barometric pressure (in millibars)

Nimbo stratus is a heavy cloud moving solidly along. Rain can be safely predicted but it is possible to fly beneath the cloud, albeit in wet and miserable conditions.

Alto cumulus or 'fair weather' cumulus below high cirrus. These clouds are relatively harmless to aeronauts and are often used by them as playgrounds.

Cumulo-nimbus (below) towering into the sky. The peaks are probably higher than 10,000 ft. No sane balloonist would fly in these conditions. The turbulence can destroy a balloon in seconds.

A winter's day when a depression and a warm front have produced 'umbrella ballooning' conditions. The solid black cloud base warns of impending rain, gusty conditions and low temperatures.

High cirrus heralds the approach of changing weather. The clouds are composed of minute ice crystals suspended in the thin atmosphere at a height of 30,000 ft or more. Usually this signals an approaching warm front some 200 miles or 10 hours behind. (Depressions in the northern hemisphere travel at about 20 mph.)

Touch-down

Good landing sites are not always easy to find in the intensively cultivated agricultural areas of Europe. In the Loire valley of France valuable vineyards are more frequent than open meadows. In Britain one has to be aware of race horses, herds of cattle and other livestock. A landing in a Dutch tulip field could create an expensive retrieve problem. In the wide open space of America the hazards are different: when attempting to land in the desert terrain around Albuquerque pilots have to avoid giant thorn bushes, cacti and sometimes even rattlesnakes.

The characteristics of an ideal landing site are similar to those of a launch field. It should be grassy, or at least free of crops, rocks and livestock, with no downwind obstacles. The choice of landing site is made from the air, and as balloons generally travel in straight lines the pilot's ability to steer is a critical factor. Some pilots boast of always landing beside an access road—and *never* in a muddy field.

The balloonist makes a landing approach in a similar way to an aircraft pilot, lowering the machine in a gradual, controlled descent path towards the chosen site. Frequent, short bursts of heat are used to control the rate of descent. Most pilots claim they can sense the balloon's inertia through their feet and are able to judge the rate of climb or fall by feel. A controlled rate of descent is between 400 and 800 feet per minute, slowing to a vertical touchdown speed of about 100 fpm. The basket jolts lightly on the ground, drags briefly as the pilot spills the air from the rip panel in the balloon's crown and comes to rest usually 10 to 20 yards after the initial touchdown.

On a calm day a clear run of at least 60 yards is needed to leave room for the deflated envelope. On a windy day landing may require up to 300 yards of clear field, or some shelter to shield the balloon from the full force of the wind. Landings go wrong when a balloon hits the ground in a high wind with too much vertical descent speed. This is transformed into horizontal motion and the ensuing drag is lengthened considerably. A learner pilot who lands with such a bump is likely to lose his grip on the rip line at the vital moment of impact,—and the balloon ploughs across the field, under full, billowing sail.

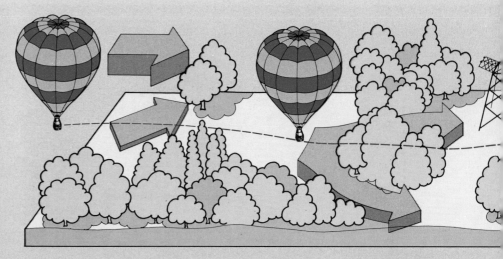

The pilot with thoughts of landing in a 10-knot wind starts his planning 10-20 minutes, one to three miles, before touchdown. From 1,000 ft he anticipates the wind direction and selects one or two fields which give a choice of overshoot alternatives, memorizing them visually; there will be little time for consulting maps.

Descending slowly, the pilot steers for the first choice field; at 500 ft the flight path seems clear of obstructions. . . .
But the descent is too fast. Trees intervene. Climbing, the pilot swings right of his expected course. He quickly sinks back down into a small valley and goes farther left to avoid more trees. To his horror he sees power lines and climbs rapidly to avoid them. This time he stays high to pass over livestock

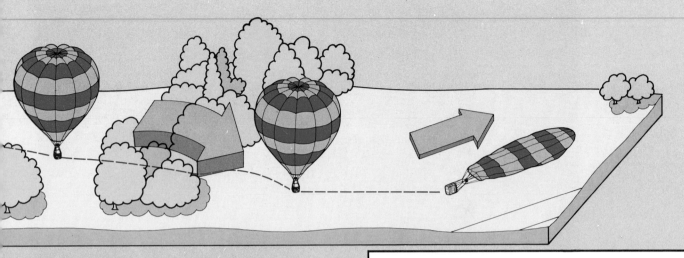

in the field behind the power lines. The pilot sees the animals following him and knows they are no longer scared, so it is safe to descend; he won't incur the wrath of a farmer. He is now back on track for the original landing site.

Coming low over the trees he makes use of their shelter and gradually descends to land close to the road where the retrieve crew is waiting.

Wind Shadow
The balloon is fast approaching a coastline. This field is the last chance to land. The pilot has to clip tree-tops, venting as he comes into the lee side of trees, to land in the wind shadow. The space he has to land in is about equal to the height of the trees.

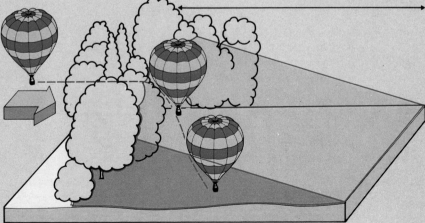

A balloon pilot's classic dilemma—as he makes an approach to land he finds he is moving across the field pattern, rather than along it. In this case (right) the balloon is heading towards the top right-hand corner. The narrowness of each strip makes the selection difficult and as the fuel runs out the choice of landing site is governed by financial considerations; the cost of damaging the wheat must be weighed against the cost of sugar beet.

Large balloons take a long time to land. The enormous AX9 comes gradually to a halt as the rip panel is opened.

All pilots dread landing in a field of crops, miles from a road. It does no good for relationships with farmers, who tend to 'shoot on sight', and recovery is difficult.

On hard ground a 20mph landing can feel like 60mph. The pilot who flew the Sky Chariot into a tree escaped unhurt. The envelope was blown off undamaged and the gondola lowered on ropes. Balloon accidents are rarely serious and often funny (if only in retrospect).

Go fetch

A balloon cannot be flown without a team who keep their feet very much on the ground.

The ground crew looks after the balloon before it ever takes to the air—refuelling the cylinders, unloading, laying out the envelope and inflating. Then, while the aerostat floats towards its unknown destination, the crew members work on the pursuit and safe retrieval of balloon and flight crew.

There are many people involved in ballooning who have never flown. Wives, girlfriends, neighbours and casual acquaintances, who have no desire to risk their own limbs, turn out week after week, throughout the year, to maintain their pilots' machines with tender care. It sounds like a thankless task but retrieving is a popular and ever-growing aspect of ballooning—so much so that there is now a retrievers' union in the USA, known as the United Aerostat Chasers International Union.

Once a balloon is in the air, travelling as the crow flies, the hapless ground crew have to negotiate a maze of country roads and tracks, avoiding rivers, railways and major roads which often cut across the path as barriers to a successful retrieve. The crew often have to work harder than the pilot as the balloon changes course, invalidating their best map-reading efforts. While the pilot and his passengers muse on the delights of flying through a filmy sunset cloud, the retrieve crew may despair as the balloon disappears from view behind a dark streak which is that same cloud.

Navigation by map is an aspect of the retrieval exercise but more important is the instinct of an expert crew who will sense a balloon's slightest change of course and race ahead, to pause only yards from where the balloon crosses the path of the van. These moments provide the retrieve crew's satisfaction as experience, instinct, luck and driving skill come together. Most often, though, there is little time for self-congratulation as the balloon flies over and continues on its way. During the post-flight debriefing, 'moments' in the retrieve are discussed as often as those of the flight. For retrieving is an art and a sport which brings its own satisfaction.

One of the biggest contributions a sponsor can make is to provide a chase vehicle. In Europe, vans are commonly used to carry dismantled rigs. American pick-up trucks carry baskets complete with burner frames.

Vehicles are often fitted with two-way radios to maintain contact with balloons. Four-wheel drive is more than useful for awkward retrieves but at some point the packed envelope will have to be man-handled. At least four strong arms are needed to lift a balloon.

First steps to flight

Flying means freedom—but although ballooning is a cheap form of aviation it is not free.

It is best to make it a family sport; the expense will look less frightening divided by a number of involved people. In Britain syndicate ownership is common, as it is with bigger boats. Start the group with one qualified pilot and the rest can learn for nothing.

As in other sports you get what you pay for. The basic model balloons are good rugged flying machines, but each manufacturer promotes packages of optional extras which enhance the appeal of the machine. Sybaritic friends may be turned off by a raw wicker basket, but trim it in luxuriant suede, lacquer the cane, hide the gas bottles behind soft attractive padding and there's a very different ambience.

The average economy balloon is equipped with a single burner quite powerful enough for leisurely Sunday afternoon flying. But fit a double unit and the balloon's heart is transformed into the equivalent of a racing motor.

Instruments tell you, at a glance, what you have learned to feel in your feet. They improve the accuracy of flying and enable you to monitor performance. To fly at 1,500 fpm upwards or downwards is ballooning's equivalent of 'doing the ton', but you will never know you've done it without a variometer. With an altimeter you can tell when you have reached oxygen level—another 'ton up'. The thermistor tells you how hot you are, which is worth knowing since each degree above 110°C (230°F) costs money in envelope degradation.

A fan helps to inflate the balloon without the risk of a raw flame burning the envelope. And that helps social relationships, since a relaxed pilot tends to shout less at his crew.

Such equipment is worthwhile but by no means necessary. If you can afford it, get it. If not, then buy it over a period of time. Balloons are now recognized by finance companies as objects with resale value like cars, and credit is probably available from your local manufacturer or dealer who will always help you spend money.

Instruction in flying your new machine should be cheap; there are always pilots willing to train you in return for free flights. Once you have gained the licence, you can fly from your own private launch site or you can meet other 'balloonatics' on common ground. Throughout the year there are regular meets at local, national and international level, taking place all over the world, all open to newcomers.

Costs of operating a balloon (based on Thunder catalogue prices 1980)

	Year 1	Year 2	Year 3	Year 4
New balloon AX7 (3/4 people)	$11,000 £4,000			
Optional equipment	$4,000 £2,000			
Flying lessons	$2,000 £1,000			
Flying costs/ 100 hours	$3,000 £1,500	$3,000 £1,500	$3,000 £1,500	$3,000 £1,500
Insurance (comprehensive)	$1,200 £500	$1,200+ £500+	$1,200+ £500+	$1,200+ £500+
Replacement envelope				$7,000 £3,000
Total cost	$21,200 £9,000	$4,200 £2,000	$4,200 £2,000	$11,200 £5,000
Average annual cost over four years				$10,200 £4,500

Aerostats are forgiving machines and many balloonists will say that they found it easier to learn to fly than to drive a car. The first technique to master is inflating the balloon. Then, curiously, there is often a crisis of confidence.... Will that big bag, which I just filled with hot nothing, actually carry people, particularly me, into the sky?

In the event, the first few hours of mistakes under instruction are generally more amusing than frightening or dangerous. The 'natural' fliers have a sense of balance, or feel for what's going on; and the instructor will vary his methods to suit the novice's degree of perception.

The learner must be aware that the machine will tend to fly horizontally on an oscillating path, similar to the shape of a sine curve. To fly straight and level he must burn just as the balloon reaches the crest of a wave, before the contained air cools. Experienced pilots will explain that a balloon can fly hot or cold at the same altitude: a hot balloon is always about to climb a cold balloon will descend. Climbing is easy—the sky is the limit. Descending is not so simple. The ground is hard and prickly, containing obstructing trees and power wires, and it has to be approached cautiously. A pilot must also know when it is necessary to overshoot.

During training, an understanding of theories is acquired. Atmospheric effects, weather forecasting and navigation are studied and a checkout flight with an examiner precedes the solo flight.

The first solo is an unforgettable experience. You are alone, in the basket of a balloon, climbing skywards. The balloon is flying like a feather because with only one occupant it is underloaded. For the first time there is no one to confide in, no one to advise 'burn' at the last moment. But the trepidation is followed by exhilaration as you realize that the balloon is responding to your control.

My own solo, late on a summer evening, was hardly a solo at all for I was accompanied throughout the flight by a pigeon which rested contentedly on the crown of the balloon. It gave me a perhaps undeserved confidence that this bird put its trust in me, a learner.

Procedures, methods of training and legal requirements vary from country to country but the best move a total newcomer can make is to contact a balloon club or federation, either direct or through the national aero club. They will supply information on:

Manufacturers
A balloon manufacturer or his local dealer will be able to arrange complete training facilities for customers.

Balloon schools
Professional instruction from a balloon school or a manufacturer is expensive but efficient. Training is usually completed in 10 to 14 days and includes both practical and theoretical tuition.

Instructors
In most countries instructor ratings are awarded to pilots of sufficient skill and experience. All or part of the training flights may have to be carried out with an instructor. If you have friends who are experienced pilots then this obviously cuts the cost of learning.

Examiners
Appointed by the balloon club on behalf of the national aviation authority to certify that a student has achieved a safe level of competence in practical and theoretical instruction. The number of flying hours needed before a licence can be granted is between 10–20, depending on the country.

Reading material
Still a rare commodity since ballooning is such a new sport, but the national balloon clubs will issue basic data. Manufacturers publish flight manuals. Information on air law, weather and navigation is the same as that used for light aviation.

Medical requirements
They vary enormously, but medical standards are much lower than for aircraft licences. Glasses or contact lenses can be worn, even colour blindness is not a problem. You can be asthmatic or only have one eye. People fly with wooden legs.

The best source of information is a local balloon pilot. Balloonists' addresses are published by the national club. Phone up a pilot and invite yourself to help fly his balloon. Buy him a drink. He is the person who will be most important to you as you buy a balloon and learn to fly it.

	Exams	Flying hours under instruction	Check out flight	Solo
USA	written & oral	10	Yes	Must ascend to over 2,500 ft. 1 hr duration
UK	written	12	Yes min. 30 mins	Yes min. 30 mins
Holland	oral	20	to include one difficult landing	to at least 3,000 ft.
Germany & Austria	written	20 (including 5 at 20°C, 5 at 0°C or less)	50 take-offs & landings	No
France	written	10	to at least 3,000 ft.	2 flights
Denmark	written	8 ascents of 2 hours	to 10,000 ft.	Yes
Sweden	written	12	Yes	Yes min. 1 hr

Civil Aviation Authority (UK)
Curriculum for Flight Training Exercises

1. Familiarisation with balloon, equipment and controls.
2. Rigging the balloon for flight.
3. Preparation for flight:-
   (a) Obtaining met. forecast and appreciation of conditions.
   (b) Passenger and crew briefing.
   (c) Check of down-wind hazards.
4. Inflation.
5. Pre-take-off checks.
6. Take-off:-
   (a) Normal.
   (b) Light, from shelter in moderate wind.
7. Level flight; effect of burner.
8. Climbing and descending; use of vent.
9. Approach and overshoot from low level.
10. Use of maps; appreciation of controlled airspace.
11. Landing using vent.
12. Landing using rip panel.
13. Approach and overshoot from high level.
14. Pilot light failure; emergency procedure.
15. Flight in wind greater than 12 knots.
16. Fast climb and descent.
17. Fuel management.
18. Use of Trail Rope and Handling Line.
19. Tethered flights.

Airmanship and Balloon System Examinations

Pre-inflation checks; post inflation checks; crew and passenger briefing; pre-flight checks; in-flight checks.

Criteria for take-off sites; weather conditions.

Launching; in-flight and landing hazards and precautions; problems of intermediate touch-downs.

Flying in convection – hazards and precautions.

Landing; criteria for landing fields; crowd control; relationship with landowners.

Emergency procedures in event of failure of burner system or pilot system. Premature descents in down draught. Miscalculation of take-off angle or approach glidepath. Emergency use of burner, ripping line, trailrope, ballast.

Canopy controls. Definition and purpose of primary and secondary structural elements. Permissible damage.

Propane. Properties in liquid and gaseous form. Ground handling and transfer. Storage, fire prevention and fighting. Laws and regulations.

Burners. Principles of operation; main elements and controls; output in different ambient conditions; care and maintenance.

High rise research

'The experiments having satisfied me, I laid aside the oar, and again had recourse to my bottle; this I emptied to the health of my friends … [and] sat down and wrote four pages of desultory observations.'

Even the earliest balloonists considered the furthering of science to be one of their prime objectives, and most of them carried out 'experiments' of one kind or another. But as this extract from Lunardi's *Account* suggests, the mysteries of science did not always hold the balloonists' undivided attention and, on occasion, their powers of observation were rather blurred. Most early experiments were aeronautical, as balloonists tried out means of propelling or steering their craft.

The first truly scientific ascent was undertaken by Joseph Gay-Lussac and Jean Baptiste Biot for the Académie Française in 1804, to verify the extravagant claims of Etienne Robertson, a notorious showman, who had claimed to have observed the Earth's magnetic pull diminish at high altitude. Robertson also maintained that there was no air in the higher regions of the atmosphere, but only what he enigmatically described as 'fumes'. The two French balloonists found that air humidity decreased at higher levels and that the Earth's magnetic pull remained constant. On a later ascent, Gay-Lussac collected air in vacuum flasks at an altitude of 19,000 ft.

James Glaisher, head of the Greenwich Observatory in London, made over 30 ascents with Henry Coxwell in the *Mammoth* between 1862 and 1866, during which he investigated the composition of the atmosphere and studied the physiological effect of altitude on animals. On the first of these ascents, on September 5, 1862, the two aeronauts made a dangerous 'discovery': hypoxia, or oxygen starvation, which was to provide a physiological barrier to man's penetration of the atmosphere for 70 years to come. Glaisher collapsed over the controls at a height of about 33,000 ft but Coxwell, on the verge of unconsciousness, managed to valve off some gas, causing the balloon to descend.

Meanwhile, valuable scientific experiments were being undertaken at lower altitudes. In 1850 a scientific ascent from the Paris Observatory made the first polarimetric observations, as well as establishing the existence of ice crystals suspended in the atmosphere, thus explaining the composition of cirrus clouds. In 1874 two aeronauts, Sivel and Croce-Spinelli, equipped with oxygen and nitrogen to ward off hypoxia, rose to 22,000 ft in the *Zenith*, and took basic spectroscopic readings. On a flight in 1875 the *Zenith* stayed aloft for 35 hours, enabling prolonged meteorological readings to be made. Three weeks later the balloon ascended once more, with Sivel, Croce-Spinelli and the famous balloonist Gaston Tissandier on board. The balloon reached a height of 25,000 ft, an altitude which proved too great for two of the aeronauts, and Tissandier alone recovered consciousness.

At the turn of the century two Germans, Arthur Berson and Rheinard Süring, both professors at the meteorological institute in Berlin, ascended successfully in the balloon *Prussia* to 35,433 ft, in an open basket, inhaling oxygen through mouthpieces. Their achievement was not to be surpassed until Auguste Piccard penetrated the stratosphere in 1931 and carried out scientific measurements of cosmic rays at an altitude of 52,000 ft.

Piccard, of course, was the first to fly enclosed in a pressurized gondola and, in the years

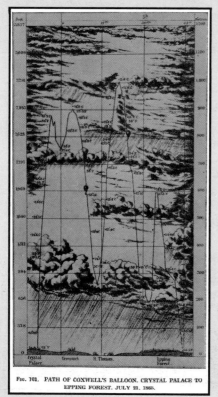

FIG. 101. PATH OF COXWELL'S BALLOON. CRYSTAL PALACE TO EPPING FOREST. JULY 21. 1868.

immediately following his flight, several other attempts were made on the altitude record. That established by the crew of *Explorer II* at 74,185 ft was the most impressive.

In 1954, at the suggestion of Piccard, Audouin Dollfus ascended into the stratosphere to carry out an astronomical observation. His extremely light aluminium gondola—the walls were only 1.2 millimetres thick—was equipped with sophisticated telescopic equipment, yet weighed only 230 lb. He gained his lift from 150 meteorological sounding balloons, strung out along one-third of a mile of cable. The ascent, made at night, was a complete success; Dollfus reached 40,000 ft and made valuable observations of Venus and the Moon. Later daylight ascents in 1956 and 1957 gave rise to important discoveries about the sun's granulations.

Soon after World War II polythene became available for balloon construction and revolutionized scientific ascents. This exceptionally light and relatively cheap material made possible the manufacture of large balloons that could reach altitudes of 100,000 ft—far higher than aircraft of the time. Now balloons could reach into space itself, and they were soon being used to test the equipment that was to take man on the next stage of his journey to the stars.

On June 2, 1957, Captain Joseph Kittinger of the US Air Force rose to 90,000 ft in a 168,000 cu ft balloon before parachuting back to earth—the highest jump ever at that time. Its purpose was to test the Beaupre parachute, designed to counter the devastating rotation speed of 465 rpm to which a man in free fall is subjected at that altitude. Kittinger made a series of breathtaking jumps, some from over 100,000 ft, during which he also tested the new MC3 pressure suit and gained often alarming first-hand experience of the conditions that would confront space crews during re-entry.

In the same year *Man High II* ascended to 105,000 ft carrying Major D. Simons enclosed in a tiny capsule, less than 3 ft in diameter and 8 ft long, to test the psychological and physiological pressures that astronauts would encounter in future space exploration. The flight was intended to last 24 hours, but severe storms and turbulence extended it to 32 hours 10 minutes, during which Simons continued to make meterological and astronomical observations.

Capable of providing platforms for observation at high altitude, manned balloons retain their usefulness for scientists in astrophysics, meteorology, astronomy and pollution control. In an ironic echo of Gay-Lussac's collection of air samples from the atmosphere on the second scientific balloon ascent ever, in 1976 the pressurized balloon *America* entered the smoke plume rising from the Four Corners Power Station at Farmington, New Mexico, to take samples for the Environmental Improvement Agency. Unlike Lussac's samples, which were found to contain pure, unadulterated air, the modern samples must have been heavily laced with Etienne Robertson's 'fumes'.

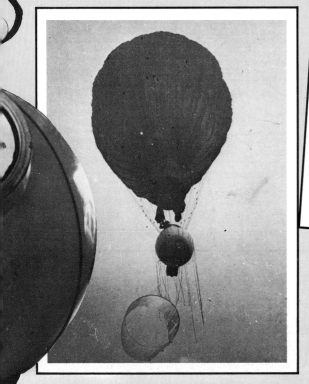

Prof. Piccard's stratospheric balloon and gondola (left) which he flew in 1931 and 1932. Above the gondola is an emergency parachute; below it hangs a drift indicator.

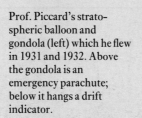

A pre-flight inspection for *Explorer II*, sponsored by the National Geographic Society. Settle and Fordney (below) emerge from their gondola in New Jersey after their 1933 altitude record flight.

149

Thousands of pieces of space junk are still whirling around the globe or heading for deep space—a scrapyard in the sky which has been added to almost daily since the 1960s space race. It is less well known that the atmosphere is also regularly being stocked with a much simpler form of conventional technology—high altitude balloons.

The most commonly launched aerostats of any kind are the 'radio sonde' weather balloons sent up by meteorologists across the world. Each day, several are launched from every major airport, accounting for thousands of balloons per day. They fly to about 60,000 ft before bursting. These lower atmosphere balloons are of similar construction to their stratospheric counterparts. Their size ranges from 4 ft to 10 ft depending on the weight of the transponder being carried to relay the weather information.

Space balloons have been in regular use since the 1950s, when companies like Schjeldahl and General Mills were building 'small' models capable of lifting 600 lb loads over 20 miles into the sky. The demands of research, defence and communications called for larger balloons to climb higher, with bigger payloads. Today balloons of 10 million cu ft can carry a ton or more of equipment 30 miles high, more reliably and more cheaply than conventional satellites.

These 'zero pressure' balloons, made of polythene, are designed so that only a small fraction of the total envelope volume is filled with helium. As the balloon rises into the thinner air of the stratosphere the gas gradually expands to fill the entire envelope, displacing sufficient air to continue lifting the payload. When float altitude is reached, excess gas vents away to minimize surface stress on the extremely lightweight material.

These balloons have a limited flight duration since the gas escapes as solar radiation makes it expand during the day; in the cool of the night it contracts, causing loss of altitude. Super-pressure balloons are being designed to withstand the stresses set up by the expanding gas. At present the most advanced high altitude technology comes from Southampton University in England. The work is on automatic ballasting systems which reduce the gross balloon weight by approximately eight per cent prior to each sunset. Thus the balloons can now maintain float altitude for up to a week.

During the 1970s, while several balloonists were being rescued from the Atlantic Ocean after attempts to cross from west to east, the Southampton team was unceremoniously launching balloons which flew from east to west, making use of 30-mile-high jet streams to land in America in as little as 75 hours. These completely automatic balloons carried payloads weighing the equivalent of a gondola with crew.

Satellite links maintain contact with the equipment as it disappears over the earth's horizon. This use of long-range scientific balloons is growing as more research teams appreciate the high success rate and low cost of the Southampton programme. The team plans to further extend the life of experimental balloons by the use of 'cryogenic' ballast. This means the balloons will carry liquid helium which can be released as necessary to maintain lift overnight.

As a flier of manned balloons I find the possibility of using the technology developed for unmanned flights fascinating. After all, the Japanese Fu-Gos crossed the Pacific, a distance of 6,000 miles, during World War II, and the Atlantic has now been flown. If the technology and the money could be made available to an imaginative pilot, the world could probably be circumnavigated by manned balloon.

One of the Southampton team's super-pressure balloons being inflated (left and above).

A similar, expanding polythene envelope was used to lift a manned gondola in the movie *On the Threshold of Space*.

Russians in the Antarctic (far left) and Americans aboard an aircraft carrier release meteorological balloons.

Return to the airship era?

The only large-scale operator of airships since the Zeppelin days is Goodyear, a name which to most Americans and Europeans is synonymous with airships. In its time the company has constructed 300 dirigibles, from the ill-fated *Akron* of 1931 to the modern publicity blimps like *Mayflower*, *Europa* and *Columbia*.

The blimps, seen regularly around the world on promotional flights, keep alive the dream of an airship age of skies dark with gliding, silent giants.

The reality of the Goodyear story is that the ships were never commercially successful. The Goodyear Zeppelin Corporation, wound-up in 1941, never operated a regular passenger or freight-carrying service. Goodyear's entire production from 1940 to 1960 consisted of naval airships for patrol and reconnaissance duties which, successful as they were, would not stand up to the rigours of commercial work. To operate in bad weather on long patrols is one thing; to set down and pick up on a regular basis under the same conditions is quite another.

In the early 1950s Goodyear tried to promote the use of airships by other sponsors and for a short time machines were chartered to Mobil Gas, Canada Dry and others, but the promotion was not successful and Goodyear reverted to operating the ships under their own colours.

The main blimp bases are at Wingfoot Lake, Spring, Texas, and Capena in Italy, but the ships go out on regular promotional tours, operating from mobile bases.

Over the years the Goodyear company has perfected a technique of ground handling which allows the ships to be maintained fully inflated and operational, without needing the traditional, enormous hangars.

The reinforced noses of the blimps are designed so that they can be attached to a mooring mast around which they swing with the wind as a ship swings about its anchor. Portable masts built on to road vehicles have been tried but more commonly the mast is a dismountable structure erected in the centre of an area the size of a baseball diamond. Sophisticated ground handling techniques have simplified take-off and landing procedures— when an airship is most vulnerable and dangerous.

Surprising as it may seem, gas-filled airships fly 'heavy'. Although they achieve a percentage of their lift from the gas, they rely on dynamic lift to take off and to stay in the air. In consequence most blimps do require an airfield of sorts in order to gain some lift from forward motion.

The Goodyear crews use a technique which they call the 'bounce-down' to achieve initial lift. About a dozen of the crew push down hard on the handling rail around the car making the ship sink on its wheel springs, before it bounces back into the air. Once satisfied that the ship is ballasted on an even keel, they bounce it again, with some of the crew pushing the nose up to the

correct angle. At the same time the pilot applies full power so that the ship lifts off smoothly. A German company, Westdeutsche Luftwerbung, which currently produces blimp-type airships similar to the Goodyear models, is working on the principle of using vectored thrust, from engines which can be angled, instead of the bounce-down technique.

A British company, Aerospace Developments, now re-born as Airship Developments, actually built vectored-thrust engines on their AD 500 and the pilot, an ex-Goodyear man, reported satisfactory operation with a much greater degree of control than he had ever had with a more conventional ship. The engines could be used to provide thrust for vertical take-off and additional lifting power, or a reverse thrust to draw the airship downwards. Such systems also go some way towards controlling airships in the gusty ground winds which constitute the greatest hazards to their safety.

Actual costs, per pound of weight carried/per mile of journey, are much lower for airships than for conventional aircraft. In theory, the airship can function as a 'sky-hook', running a door-to-door service. It can arrive at a parcels' sorting office in the centre of London, pick up a container of mail and deliver it two hours later to a post office in Paris, during which time conventional methods might have got the mail to the London airport cargo shed.

In practice, on a hot day in London the airship pilot would have difficulty controlling his ship in the bubbling thermals. Loading time would be prolonged as the ship idled in the sky waiting for the turbulence to die down. Once loaded, the airship might encounter a strong south-westerly headwind of 40 knots, increasing the journey time to four hours. In Paris the pilot might have to give up, or risk his ship in unfavourable, blustery conditions, flying low over the rooftops and finally delivering the mail after an exhausting eight-hour journey. This scenario is not overly pessimistic—weather conditions are impossible to predict and that simple fact exposes the fantasy behind these speculative airship freighter projects.

Many uses for airships have been envisaged, but few are practical. Some time ago it was suggested that overcrowded seaports could use freighter airships as a ship-to-shore transport system. I suspect that hovercraft might be better. Oil companies looked at the possibility of bringing North Sea gas ashore by airship using the buoyancy of the gas to support the ship, but the project was abandoned as unrealistic. There has been talk of using airships in under-developed countries to transport crops and timber across otherwise inaccessible areas, but no one has yet built an airship which is capable of undertaking these types of project. The practical problems remain unsolved. Airships are basically incompatible with the turbulent atmosphere of our planet.

There could be unspectacular applications for small 'sky-hooks' which could be controlled in average weather. There may even be a future for enormous freighters, making use of centralized docking facilities similar to those at conventional airports. But this development will take a long time and the kind of finance which only large corporations and governments are capable of raising. So far financiers have remained unconvinced.

Cameron D-96

The world's first hot-air dirigible, and for a long time the only one in production, is the Cameron D–96, first flown in public at the Icicle Meet in January 1973. Typical of Don Cameron's design approach, this simple, tough machine has an open cockpit and no frills. Power is provided by a modified Volkswagen engine mounted at the rear of the steel-framed car.

The weight of the car is carried by a load tape structure, similar to that of a balloon. Vertical and diagonal tapes are attached to the envelope surface so the hull can absorb the stress without too much distortion. When in flight the envelope is naturally pressurized by a scoop, similar to those used to inflate the tailplanes of wartime observation blimps.

The original version had only one vertical fin beneath the tail of the fuselage, since it was anticipated that at the low airspeeds for which it was designed, other fins would be of little value. After test flying, horizontal tailplanes were added, to prevent excessive nose–up attitudes when accelerating. The current model has four fins which are pressure-inflated by a non–return air duct placed in the propeller slipstream. The first models had a top speed of 8–12 knots but subsequent improvements

have raised this slightly. The D–96 is by no means an all-weather model and is usually operated on calm mornings and evenings only.

The seating in the open cockpit is side by side, on a bench fitted with safety belts. The controls consist of engine and burner throttles, rudder and rip panel. The rudder is attached to a rope which runs through the car on pulleys. Changes of direction are achieved by pulling the rope from left to right or vice versa. Maintaining course can be hard work in the freezing draught of an exposed cockpit.

Since there are no elevator controls the only method of climbing or descending is to make use of the burner as in a standard balloon.

Raven Starship

The most sophisticated attempt yet at the production of a serious thermal airship is the Raven Starship, first flown in 1975 and developed with the help of Kurt Ruenzi, the Alpine balloonist. The craft has an approximate 'fineness' (length to height) ratio of 2.2 : 1 being 120 ft long, 56 ft high and 48 ft wide with a design volume of 140,000 cu ft. It has an estimated speed of 25 mph and a gross lift of 2,100 lb.

Like the Cameron D–96, the Starship uses a propane-powered Volkswagen engine to provide

the motive power. A secondary fan gives more control of pressurization to maintain envelope shape.

When the machine was test flown in Switzerland it crashed. The car was redesigned and rebuilt, prior to its return to the USA. The car is suspended in conventional blimp fashion from twin catenary curtains which run along the backbone of the ship, where a Velcro rip panel is also located for rapid deflation when necessary. The Starship has four inflated control surfaces, with an operational rudder on the lower vertical fin and movable elevator planes. With speeds in excess of 20 knots these surfaces provide the pilot with good control responses.

The Cameron D–96 climbs by heat alone; the Raven Starship has an alternative method. The pilot can climb dynamically by increasing speed and making use of the elevators on the tail plane. In theory this makes the craft more controllable, but in practice it may create undesirable, internal air movement. Certainly, flying the Raven ship is not a one-man job.

The only full-sized competitor is the Busch airship, but as Raven have only produced one Starship to date, there is some doubt as to its commercial potential.

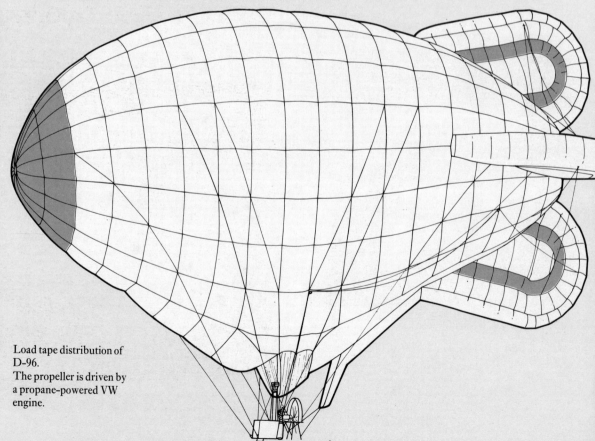

Load tape distribution of D-96.
The propeller is driven by a propane-powered VW engine.

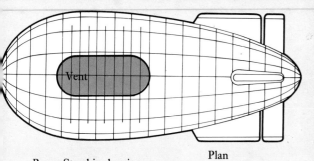

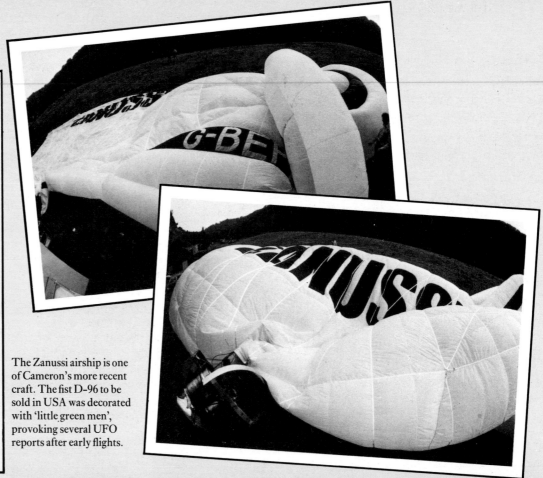

Raven Starship showing vent panel and catenary suspension curtains.

Plan

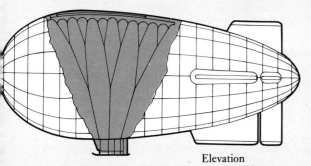

Elevation

The Zanussi airship is one of Cameron's more recent craft. The fist D-96 to be sold in USA was decorated with 'little green men', provoking several UFO reports after early flights.

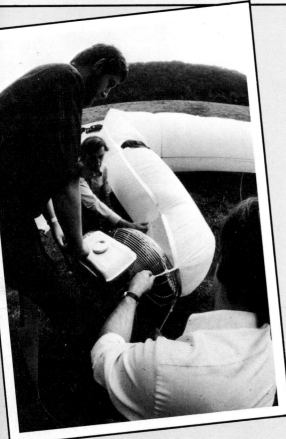

A hazard of being an airship designer is the inevitable association with the cranks who often appear as apologists for these beautiful, improbable machines. Some of the airship companies which offer nuclear-powered or solar-powered impossibilities are suspect. Their only successes are with press releases and attempts to divert research money into dubious aspects of LTA (lighter-than-air) technology.

Barnes Wallis, the British aeronautical inventor and designer of the R100, a successful airship, dismissed the idea of latterday airships. 'They belong to the '20s and '30s'. End of story. But airships can fly; *Graf Zeppelin* and dozens of Goodyear blimps have shown that. They are safe too, and may yet have a role to play as fuel becomes scarcer.

The state of airship design has remained unchanged for many years, except in theory, because the big aircraft manufacturers are not interested, even though there are some truths discernible among the futuristic fantasies. Goodyear, the only airship company with a track record, regularly submits designs to NASA, but so far no airships have materialized.

The US Navy blimps, sophisticated, comfortable craft, were phased out only because satellites could perform their surveillance role more economically. But satellites cannot patrol the seas to stop illicit fishing or to guard isolated oil rigs. In such guardian roles the airship has already proven its ability to remain on station, whatever the weather—in the 1950s naval airships remained airborne for up to 11 days. If airships are to be revived it would be for such unspectacular applications.

I believe that airships will never return as carriers of cargo or passengers on the scale of the 1930s. They are simply too big and too unwieldly, too slow and too vulnerable to the power of the atmosphere. There have been grandiose projects for carrying 500 tons at speeds of 100 mph with airships of 30 million cu ft (over five times the size of *Hindenburg*). That is fantasy at work. But the already successful smaller craft of under 1 million cu ft have a more realistic future.

Aerocrane

One of the more intriguing variants of the airship concept is the relatively new one of 'sky-hooks'—floating cranes. The latest American example is the Aerocrane, which the developers, All American Engineering, hope to fly in 1980, beating the rival French CNRS project into the air.

The Aerocrane is a balloon filled with gas for basic lift, supplemented by standard aero engines mounted on four short winglets. The machine is part aircraft, part helicopter and part balloon. The final product will be designed to carry up to 70 tons at speeds of up to 40 mph. Early successes with models have convinced the designers that the project is feasible.

Aereon

The Aereon Corporation, formed in 1959, revived the name and concept of the Andrews airship. The first machine, the triple-hulled *Aereon III*, never flew and, as in so many airship projects, suffered a ground accident. The next, *Aereon ZC*, looking like a 'deltoid pumpkin seed', does fly. Interestingly, it has flown under dynamic lift only, without deriving any lift from gas since the ball was left unfilled. New projects include the Aereon 340—some 340 ft long and 250 ft wide. Like the Megalifter it is designed to carry six fully loaded trailers, and operate with a crew of only five. The craft weighs approximately the same as the air it displaces. The weight of cargo is lifted, as with an aircraft, by dynamic force.

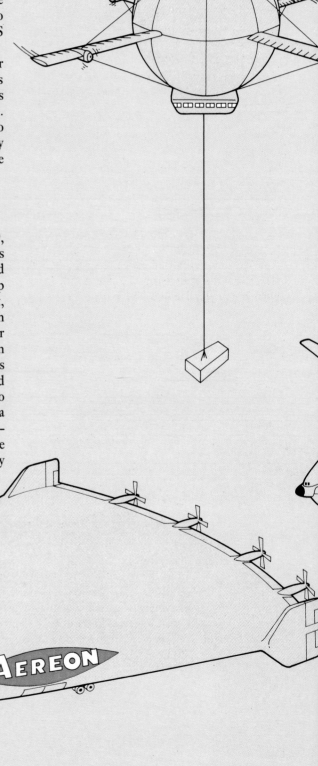

Skyship

A design for a lens-shaped, flying saucer airship produced by Skyship Transport Ltd, with design help from Imperial College, London, and the British Hovercraft Corporation. A prototype, 30 ft in diameter, has flown in the old airship sheds at Cardington.

The Skyship is primarily envisaged as a helium-supported machine with a container core for freight and passengers; lift is to be derived from dynamic as well as aerostatic properties.

Megalifter

The proposed machine is 650 ft long—part aircraft, part airship with STOL (short take-off and landing) capabilities. An airport would be required.

The machine is designed to cruise at altitudes of up to 18,000 ft, and at speeds from 75 mph to 200 mph. The potential range is 8,000 miles, with a flight duration of 60 hours or more, and a staggering payload of 400,000 lb.

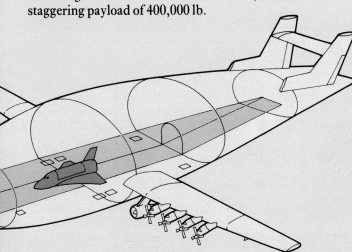

Heavy Lifter

The Goodyear Heavy Lifter, designed for NASA, combines features of airships and helicopters. The airship's buoyancy would lift its own weight. The outboard helicopter units are intended to provide additional lift for military or civilian cargoes of up to 250 tons.

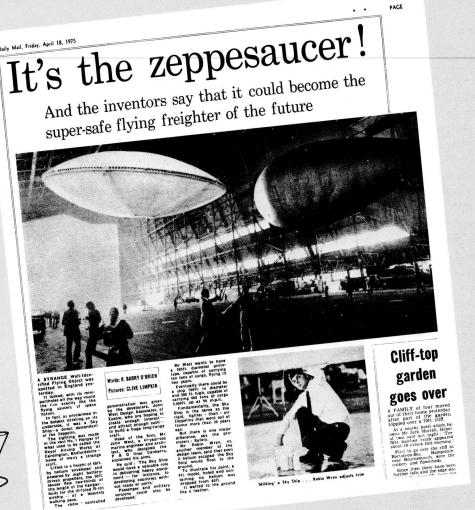

Daily Mail, Friday, April 18, 1975

It's the zeppesaucer!

And the inventors say that it could become the super-safe flying freighter of the future

A STRANGE Well-Identified Flying Object was spotted in England yesterday.

It looked, with its miniportholes all the way round the r.m. exactly like the flying saucers of space fiction.

In fact, as proclaimed in the boldest lettering on its underside, it was a Sky Ship—a direct descendant of the Zeppelin.

The sighting was made in the vast No. 1 Hangar of the Royal Airship Works at Cardington, Bedfordshire—home of many a strange craft.

Lifted to a height of 40ft, by helium 'envelopes' and powered by eight battery-driven propellers, the 30ft saucer flew two-thirds of the length of the hangar—built for the ill-fated R-101 airship—at a leisurely walking pace.

The radio - controlled

Words: R. BARRY O'BRIEN
Pictures: CLIVE LIMPKIN

demonstration was given by the developers, West Design Associates, of Epsom, who are hoping to create enough interest—and attract enough cash—to build a huge long-range craft.

Head of the firm, Mr John West, a 47-year-old marine engineer and architect, who designed the P & O liner Canberra, explained his aims.

He said : 'The Sky Ship would have a valuable role in delivering heavy equipment — for instance, to developing countries without roads or ports.'

'Passenger and military versions could also be developed.'

Mr West wants to have a 200ft. diameter prototype, capable of carrying ten tons of cargo, flying in two years.

Eventually there could be a ship 700ft. in diameter and 200 ft. high, capable of carrying 400 tons of cargo 5,000ft. up at 90 m.p.h.

Fundamentally, the Sky Ship is the same as the rigid, lighter - than - air Zeppelins that went out of favour more than 30 years ago.

But there is one major difference, say the promoters. Safety.

Mr Robin Wren, 43, another member of the design team, said that even if helium escaped the Sky Ship would float to the ground.

To illustrate his point, a 4ft. model, holed and containing no helium was dropped from 40ft. It wafted to the ground like a feather.

'Milking' a Sky Ship . . . Robin Wren adjusts trim

Cliff-top garden goes over

A FAMILY of four moved out of their home yesterday after part of the garden toppled over a 70ft. cliff.

At a nearby hotel which he owns Mr Jack Murrell, father of two, said last night : 'The first hairline crack appeared about 10 o'clock this morning.'

First to go over the cliff at Barton-on-Sea, near Bournemouth, Hampshire, were the rockery and flowerbeds.

Since then there have been further falls and the edge was

A graceful cigar-shaped airship, filled with hot air, would tend to stand on its end like an inflated flag-pole as soon as the nose was inclined upwards. Hot air, unlike gas, is never of a uniform density and the hottest of it would rush to the highest point, lifting the nose until the ship settled in a vertical position. The problem is being overcome by designers who favour short, stubby machines.

The pioneer of hot-air dirigible design who discovered this truth is Anthony Smith. In 1964 there were few builders of conventional hot-air balloons and no one had yet tried to make hot-air dirigibles. Early that year Smith returned from a visit to Raven Industries in Dakota, inspired to adapt the hot-air technology to the design of an airship.

The subsequent Warm Airship Project (WASP) was a joint venture. Malcolm Brighton, builder of Britain's first hot-air balloon, designed WASP but when it was taken for testing at the Cardington hangar the hot-air craft was declared a fire risk and could not be inflated in the vicinity of under-floor hydrogen pipes. The appropriately waspish-looking craft was eventually inflated over a sandpit, where it also ended its short career.

The long, thin ship suffered badly from internal surges of air and was highly unstable. It never did fulfil the expectations of the inventors, whose enthusiasm and finance eventually dried up.

Anthony Smith returned to more conventional gas ballooning after the WASP project, but he still had a dream which could only be realized with a dirigible airship. Smith is a traveller and romantic who has written a best-selling book on flight over Africa. His new dream was to fly over the Amazonian forest, landing in otherwise unreachable places. The only possible way to make such an expedition was by airship.

The problems of controlling the WASP had left Smith convinced that gas was the medium to use. Inspired by Santos-Dumont, the popular Brazilian character who 70 years before had manoeuvred his hydrogen-filled gasbags over the rooftops of Paris, Smith's second airship took shape. The helium-filled dirigible, which took the name of the pioneer aeronaut, was powered by twin Wankel rotary engines driving ducted fans. It was squat and dumpy but it flew successfully; it even survived one crash to be repaired and flown again. Smith's *Santos-Dumont* was probably the most successful small airship of the 1960s.

AD 500

On paper the AD 500 was full of promise (the blimp shape was reminiscent of the successful Goodyear ships); in practice, it flew once, in front of the press, and was then wrecked on its mooring mast in a storm.

The AD 500, brainchild of Roger Mark, the director of Aerospace Developments, included much up-to-the-minute technology. The 180,000 cu ft envelope was made of plastic laminate by the French Aerazur company. The car was fibreglass and the ship was powered by two Porsche engines. These drove enclosed propellers which could be moved to alter the angle of thrust—a facility which allowed the ship to take off vertically without the need for a runway.

The company folded when the prototype was lost. But the idea persists. The builders are now apparently under contract to the Royal Navy to build a reconnaissance ship on the same lines.

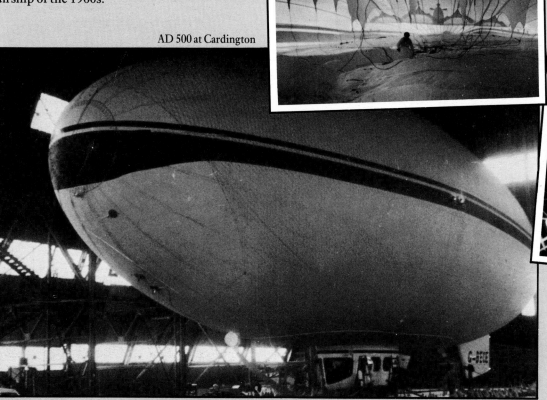

WASP on the drawing board

AD 500 at Cardington

Smith's *Santos-Dumont*

Thunder

Thunder Balloons began with airships. My partner Tom Donnelly became interested in balloon-building as a way to find the means of producing a dirigible.

The original intention, to build a 150,000 cu ft pressurized ship, powered by a Lycoming aircraft engine, has been largely abandoned. A 40 ft-long test model, built in early 1979, showed that we could successfully control the internal air surge which had confounded the WASP, but construction difficulties prompted us to re-think the project.

Construction has finally started on Thunder's own *Santos-Dumont*, a small one-man hot-airship designed specifically for advertising and promotion work. The hull is pressurized by a secondary engine as are those of the Starship and Busch craft.

The ship has a volume of 60,000 cu ft, making it the smallest hot-airship yet. It is powered by a 500cc water-cooled engine driving a ducted fan. The length to height ratio is 3.5:1, like Goodyear's blimps, and the flight duration should be about two hours. A prototype should be flying in mid-1980.

Busch Airship

When World Balloons of Albuquerque wanted to test the advertising potential of an airship they were frustrated to find that none was available. They decided to make their own. An envelope was commissioned from George Stokes, and a car built to match it.

The resulting 'Busch Thermal Airship' is the largest and most ambitious hot-airship project to date. The pressurized envelope has a volume of 229,000 cu ft giving a theoretical lift of 4,000 lb gross. The power plant is a Lycoming 180 hp engine and the hot-air burners are two Raven 'square shooters'. The length to height ratio, 175 ft to 50 ft, is 3.5:1, similar to a Goodyear blimp and more cigar-shaped than any previous hot-airship. The theoretical forward speed is 35 mph.

The machine is still in the early stages of development. World Balloons have been prepared to risk ridicule in an effort to prove the potential of such vehicles. A prospective customer will need $250,000 to purchase one.

Boland Albatross

First inflated on October 8, 1975, this airship is one of many splendid creations of the husband and wife team of Brian and Kathy Boland. They have to their credit a range of balloons, from one-man types that pack into suitcases, through to a larger variety featuring a small Messerschmitt 'bubble car' which can double as balloon gondola or road vehicle.

The *Albatross*, however, was the first Boland attempt at a thermal airship. The first model was powered by a 40 hp Rockwell engine complementing three independent 8 million BTU burners. The ship had an approximate volume of 140,000 cu ft; it was 112 ft long, 50 ft wide and 60 ft high.

The initial model had a smaller rudder and a stabilizing fin and was capable of carrying three or four people with comparative ease. The ship has since been improved by the addition of a large, slipstream-inflated lower fin and rudder to improve steering.

Boland Albatross

Thunder prototype

Busch thermal airship

Appendix

HOT-AIR BALLOON RECORDS

Category	Pilot	Date of record	Location	Altitude feet	(metres)	Distance miles (kilometres)		Duration hours minutes
AX–1	Katherine E. Boland	November 78	USA	11,407	(3,477.00)	—		—
AX–1	Katherine E. Boland	July 78	USA	—		2.99	(4.81)	0:30:05
AX–2	Katherine E. Boland	November 78	USA	11,407	(3,477.00)	—		—
AX–2	Donna Wiederkehr	March 75	USA	—		11.19	(18.01)	2:40:00
AX–3	Brian Boland	November 78	USA	15,229	(4,642.00)	—		—
AX–3	Brian Boland	August 78	USA	—		35.6	(57.30)	3:46:00
AX–4	Capt. Geoff Green	October 78	Hong Kong	22,299	(6,797.00)	—		—
AX–4	Matt H. Wiederkehr	March 73	USA	—		85.4	(137.48)	5:05:55
AX–5	Carol Davis	March 80	USA	31,791	(9,690.00)	—		—
AX–5	Simon Faithfull	November 78	UK	—		110.6	(178.00)	—
AX–5	Matt H. Wiederkehr	March 73	USA	—		—		5:05:55
AX–6	Carol Davis	March 80	USA	31,791	(9,690.00)	—		—
AX–6	Denise Wiederkehr	March 74	USA	—		229.9	(369.99)	—
AX–6	Julian R. P. Nott	April 78	UK	—		—		11:20:00
AX–7	Julian R. P. Nott	June 76	UK	37,027	(11,286.00)	—		—
AX–7	Ed Chapman	March 80	USA	—			(611.00)	—
AX–7	Ed Chapman	March 80	USA	—		—		19+ hours
AX–8	Kingswood Sprott, Jr	September 75	USA	38,789	(11,822.91)	—		—
AX–8	Ed Chapman	March 80	USA	—		379.6	(611.00)	—
AX–8	Ed Chapman	March 80	USA	—		—		19+ hours
AX–9	Chauncey M. Dunn	August 79	USA	52,998	(16,154.00)	—		—
AX–9	Ed Chapman	March 80	USA	—		379.6	(611.00)	—
AX–9	Matt H. Wiederkehr	March 74	USA	—		—		19+ hours
AX–10	Chauncey M. Dunn	August 79	USA	53,198	(16,215.36)	—		—
AX–10	Ed Chapman	March 80	USA	—		379.6	(611.00)	—
AX–10	Ed Chapman	March 80	USA	—		—		19+ hours

Category	Pilot	Date of record	Location	Altitude feet (metres)	Distance miles (kilometres)	Duration hours minutes
Hot-air/Helium						
AM–10	Donald Cameron, Christopher Davey	July 78	UK	—	2,075 (3,339.08)	96:24:00
AM–11	Donald Cameron, Christopher Davey	July 78	UK	—	2,075 (3,339.08)	96:24:00
AM–12	Donald Cameron, Christopher Davey	July 78	UK	—	2,075 (3,339.08)	96:24:00
AM–13	Donald Cameron, Christopher Davey	July 78	UK	—	2,075 (3,339.08)	96:24:00
AM–14	Donald Cameron, Christopher Davey	July 78	UK	—	2,075 (3,339.08)	96:24:00
AM–15	Donald Cameron, Christopher Davey	July 78	UK	—	2,075 (3,339.08)	96:24:00

World Hot-Air Balloon Champions

1973 Dennis Flodden (USA)
1975 David Schaffer (USA)
1977 Paul Woessner (USA)
1979 Paul Woessner (USA)

US National Champions

1963 Dick Pollard
1964 Jimmy Craig
1965 Jimmy Craig
1966 George Craig
1970 Frank Pritchard
1971 Dennis Flodden
1972 Bruce Comstock
1973 Tom Gabel
1974 Charles Ehrler
1975 David Medema
1976 Bruce Comstock
1977 Bruce Comstock
1978 Sid Cutter
1979 Bruce Comstock

British National Champions

1975 Bernard Hockley
1976 Dick Wirth
1977 Crispin Williams
1978 Alan Dorman
1979 Crispin Williams

Manufacturers
USA

Adams Balloon Loft, Inc.
P.O. Box 12168
Atlanta
Georgia 30355
(404) 261-5818

Avian Balloon Co.
South 3722 Ridgeview Drive
Spokane
Washington 99206
(509) 928-6847

Barnes Sport Balloons
Balloon Works
Rhyne Aerodrome/RFD 2
Statesville
North Carolina 28677
(704) 873-0503

Boland Balloons
Pine Drive, R.D. 2
Burlington
Connecticut 06013
(203) 673-1307

Cameron Balloons Ltd.
3600 Elizabeth Road
Ann Arbor
Michigan 48103
(313) 995-0111

Don Piccard Balloons Inc.
P.O. Box 1902
Newport Beach
California 92663
(714) 642-3545

Thunder Balloons Ltd.
Thunder Pacific
114 Sandalwood Court
Santa Rosa
California 95401
(707) 546-7124

Raven Industries
P.O. Box 1007
Sioux Falls
South Dakota 57101
(605) 336-2750

UK

Cameron Balloons Ltd.
1 Cotham Park
Bristol
0272-41455

Colt Balloons Ltd.
Maesbury Road
Oswestry
Salop
0691-2216

Thunder Balloons Ltd.
75 Leonard Street
London EC2A 4QS
01-739-0775/0776

France

Maurice Chaize
48 Rue Balay
42000 St. Etienne
(77) 33-43-76

Montgolfier Moderne
4 Rue Denis Poisson
75017 Paris
010-331-574-1997

Commercial Balloon Operators
USA

World Balloons Inc.
4800 Ewbank N.E.
Albuquerque
New Mexico 87111
(505) 293-6800

AERCO
3321 Princeton N.E.
Albuquerque
New Mexico 87107
(505) 344-5423

Airborn Pacific
P.O. Box 4887
Santa Rosa
California 95402
(070) 546-7124

UK

Lighter Than Air
24 Warstones Road
Penn
Wolverhampton
0902-334282

HABCO
14-16 Great Pulteney Street
London W1

Balloon Stable
12 Burdett Street
Ramsbury
Wiltshire
067-22-677

Balloon Federations

Federation Aviation International
6 Rue Galilee
75782 Paris
France

British Balloon and Airship Club
Kimberley House
Vaughan Way
Leicester
    Aerostat journal
    Ed: Alan Noble
    32 Greyfriars Road
    Reading

Balloon Federation of America
Suite 430, 821-15th Street N.W.
Washington DC 20005
    Ballooning journal
    Ed: Brian P.
    Lawler
    2226 Beebee Street
    San Luis Obispo
    California 93401

Club d'Intervention Aerostatique
Siege Social
12 Rue Bonaparte
75006 Paris

Danish Balloon Club
Kai Paamund (President)
Gynelhøj
Graese Skolevej 23
3600 Frederikssund

Dutch Balloon Club
K.N.V.V.L. (Balloon Section)
J. Israelsplein, 8
The Hague

Federation Française D'Aerostation
6 Rue Galilee
75782 Paris

Japan Balloon League
Saruta Building
1-4-10 Akasaka
Minato-Ku
Tokyo 107

Royal Aeroclub of Belgium
1, Rue Montyer
Bruxelles

Swedish Balloon Federation
c/o John Grubbstrom
Storskärsgatan 5
11529 Stockholm

Index

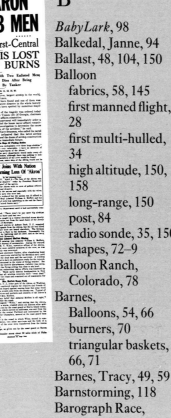

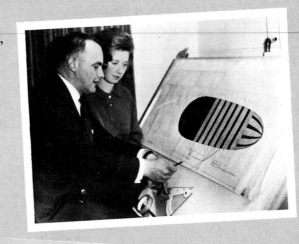

The publishers and authors wish to thank the following for their assistance in preparing this book:

Anthony Smith, Colin Mudie, Brian Boland, Hans Zoet, Darryl Gunter, Arno Seiger, Ed Yost, Tucker Comstock, Tom Shepherd, Don Piccard, Marge Ruppenthal, World Balloons Inc., Per Lindstrand, Paul Keene, Phillip Hutchins, Julian Nott, Archie Hampton, John Hampshire, Alan Depusse, Graeme Elson, Oliver Roux-Devillas, Nikon Cameras, Ben Abruzzo, Ann Kramer, Peter Wren, Goodyear Tire & Rubber Co., Robin Lee.

Additional photographs were supplied by:
Steve Moss, Tom Sage, Patrice Terrin, Simon Faithfull, Tom Donnelly, Gill Fisk, Ian Ashpole, Science Museum, Kensington, Cameron Balloons, Colt Balloons, Aspect Picture Library, B.B.C. Hulton Picture Library, Chris Butler, Colin Mudie, Larry Dale Gordon, Vince Streano, Arnold Desser, Mary Evans Picture Library, John Frost Historical Newspaper Service, Susan Griggs Agency/Michael Boys, Robert Harding Associates, John Hillelson Agency, Imperial War Museum, Kobal Collection, Ken Pilsbury, Popperfoto, Scott Polar Research Institute, Spectrum Colour Library, Zefa.
Illustrations on pp. 26–27 are Crown copyright.

The following books and magazines were particularly useful during the preparation of *Ballooning*:

Aerostat (Journal of British Balloon and Airship Club)

Airships. An Illustrated History, Henry Beaubois/Carlo Demand, Macdonald and Jane's, London

Airships for the Future, William J. White, Sterling Publishing Co. Inc., New York

Airshipwreck, Len Deighton and Arnold Schwartzman, Jonathan Cape, London

L'Atlantic en Ballon, de Saint-Sauveur/Dollfus/Fontaine, Léoréca, Paris

Back to the Drawing Board, Allen Andrews, David and Charles, Newton Abbot, UK

Ballooning (Journal of Balloon Federation of America)

Balloons, Charles Dollfus, Prentice-Hall International, London

Balloons and Airships, Lennart Ege, Blandford Press, London

The Balloon Book, Paul Fillingham, David McKay Company Inc., New York

The Blimp Book, George Hall and George Larson, Squarebooks, Mill Valley, California

The Book of Balloons, Erik Norgaard, Crown Publishers Inc., New York

The Dangerous Sort, Anthony Smith, George Allen and Unwin, London

Encyclopedia of Aviation, Reference International, London, New York

Five Weeks in a Balloon, Jules Verne, Ward Lock, London

The German Air Raids on Great Britain 1914–1918, Captain Joseph Morris, H. Pordes, London

My Airships, Alberto Santos-Dumont, Dover Publications Inc., New York

Riders of the Winds, Don Dwiggins, Hawthorn Books, New York

Extracts from *Monkey*, courtesy George Allen & Unwin. Extracts from *Five Weeks in a Balloon*, courtesy Ward Lock